INFORMATION SYSTEMS IN ARCHAEOLOGY

Roger Martlew

NEW STANDARD ARCHAEOLOGY
ALAN SUTTON

Alan Sutton Publishing Limited
17a Brunswick Road
Gloucester

First Published 1984

British Library Cataloguing in Publication Data

Information systems in archaeology.—
(New standard archaeology)
1. Archaeology—Data processing
I. Martlew, Roger   II. Series
930.1′028′54   CC80.4

ISBN 0-86299-116-1

Typesetting and origination by
Alan Sutton Publishing Limited
Photoset in 10/11 Bembo
Printed in Great Britain

ACKNOWLEDGEMENTS

All but one of the following papers were given at a weekend conference held at Leicester University in March 1982. Additional material has been provided by Cherry Lavell of the Council for British Archaeology. Ian Graham of the Institute of Archaeology, London, gave demonstrations of several micro-computer based projects throughout the weekend.

The conference was supported by a grant from the Department of Industry, as part of its Information Technology Year campaign. A mobile display unit, also part of IT82 and provided by the National Computer Centre, gave delegates a chance to examine some of the latest technology at first hand. DVW Microelectronics of Coventry demonstrated the portable 'Husky' micro-computer, designed for use in field conditions, and HB Computers of Kettering demonstrated word processing and data-base software for the Commodore Pet, along with hand held data collection devices.

The conference was organised through the Adult Education Department of Leicester University, and I am particularly grateful to Eileen Sunderland for her hard work and calmly efficient support. Illustrations for this volume have been drawn by Sue Vaughan and Martin Latham.

[CONTENTS]

PREFACE

In the seven years since the crisis in archaeological publishing was examined by a working party under Professor Frere, developments in the world of information technology have radically altered not only the solutions available, but also some of the problems. A re-appraisal is necessary of both immediate difficulties and of fundamental attitudes to how we handle information in archaeology, a fact also recognised recently by the Ancient Monuments Board in its 28th Annual Report for 1981.

The conference on information systems in archaeology, held at Leicester University in March 1982, was designed to stimulate discussion along the new paths which are now available. Speakers from outside archaeology were able to give a wider perspective to the application of information technology, and the large number of delegates from Government departments, Units and Local Authorities showed the great depth of interest amongst professional archaeologists.

During 1982 the Government launched a major awareness campaign to emphasise the importance of information technology. Most of the technology itself is not new: electronic computers have been around for over 30 years, and telecommunictions for longer. It was improvements in the power of the former and the quality of the latter, and a fall in the cost of both, which heralded what has been claimed as the most significant revolution since the harnessing of steam power.

A year after the 'Frere Report' was published the Council for British Archaeology organised a seminar on 'The Problems of Information Handling in Archaeology' (British Library Board Research and Development Report 5329, 1977). At that time it could only be anticipated that computers would play an important part in tackling the crisis in archaeological publication. A bewildering array of technology, shrouded in the unfamiliar jargon of a young subject, has burst upon the market since then. The publication crisis is still very much with us, and although the technology may appear to provide an answer, archaeologists are now faced with the burden of making the best use of new tools which, in many cases, they may not fully understand.

An important aspect of information technology is its relevance to the full range of archaeological research, and hence the title of the conference refers to 'information systems' rather than just to publishing. Information enters the system from excavations, field surveys, laboratory analyses and research studies, and flows by a number of routes to the output stage. The emphasis of the 'Frere Report' and of subsequent soul-searching in the profession has been on this last stage, where the results of archaeological research are ushered into the outside world. Information technology, however, can be applied from the initial recording stage right through to the final presentation of results, providing a common medium through all four stages of 'storage and availability of excavation data' as outlined in the 'Frere Report'.

How best to apply the new tool of information technology, and by how much it will, or ought to, change the organisation of the current 'information system', are two subjects of the important debate which will continue long after the conference. The nature of the tool implies better communication and closer co-operation between archaeologists than has so far existed. It may not be felt appropriate for every archaeologist to adopt a system which is compatible with everyone else's, but some form of central co-ordination at least may be needed to set standards and prevent the current bottlenecks from being transferred to new systems. The phrase 're-inventing the wheel' was heard many times during the conference, and the current pioneering work of individuals seems to lead inevitably to duplication of effort.

Information technology is a tool which is developing new powers at a tremendous rate, and which is steadily becoming cheaper. It will be interesting to see, in another seven years' time, the extent to which this technology has been used to improve the flow of archaeological information.

CHAPTER 1

'ONLY CONNECT'

Henry Cleere

Council for British Archaeology

My title is taken, as you will recognize, from E M Forster's *Howard's End*. It epitomizes the basic human problem, that of communication. Forster used what in more recent terminology would probably be named the 'communications gap' to describe the failure of human relationships, owing to the inability of those separated by, in this case, a class divide to find a common language that would permit them to achieve understanding: only through the non-verbal medium of music was a tenuous mutual awareness achieved between his characters, to be shattered once the directness of the emotional message of Beethoven had been blunted by the use of those most imprecise and dangerous of all tools, words and sentences.

The social message of Forster's great novel, that comprehension is only possible once effective communication has been achieved, must surely be taken as the message for this conference. Archaeologists have an immense amount to say to one another and to the world at large, but they will not derive the mutual benefit that this implies unless they can achieve effective means of communication, not across a class barrier – archaeology seems to be one of the few areas of modern society where Englishmen and women are happily not separated by birth and education – but across the barriers of specialisation that our increasingly fragmented and fissile discipline is fond of building.

I am not talking as any kind of expert in information systems in archaeology. However, as Director of the CBA I am probably uniquely placed to be able to put the technological developments that are discussed in the following papers into the framework of the overall needs of modern archaeology. The Council takes the whole of the archaeology of Britain as its province, and amongst our members are organizations and institutions representing every facet of that increasingly diversified scene. Academic research is represented by our university members, the front line of rescue archaeology by the many units and trusts up and down the country, cultural resource management by the local authority archaeological sections, and so on. What is more, we have a line to the public at large through the many mainly amateur county and local societies among our membership. As an organisation we represent archaeology in numerous ways – as a counterpart in discussions with the state archaeological services, for example, in the eyes of the media, and in joint activities with other conservation bodies concerned with the natural or the man-made environment. I am not, I hasten to add, thereby claiming any God-like omniscience, or for that matter an Olympian detachment, but merely a vantage point that may enable me to offer some general guidelines – and perhaps along with them some words of warning, since I am conscious of the fact that understandable enthusiasm on the part of our colleagues sometimes blinds them to the practical realities.

The sub-title of the Conference spoke of 'communication between archaeologists and the public'. However, the excellent programme of papers seemed to me to be concerned only with communication between archaeologists and other archaeologists, and perhaps with a few other specialists, such as planners and researchers in peripheral disciplines. In none of the paper titles was any reference made to the public as such: yet in many ways this should be the main thrust of our efforts. Modern archaeology is a costly business: it is not difficult to produce figures of ten or even twenty million pounds a year for the expenditure on archaeology in all its manifold guises – preservation, research, rescue, training, survey, collection and curation, conservation, and so on. And where do these millions come from? They come from the taxpayers and ratepayers up and down the land, and so we have a responsibility as archaeologists to make our results available to them in ways which they can readily assimilate and appreciate, otherwise we may find that we have alienated our paymasters and our funds will dry up. Already public expenditure on archaeology is being challenged by those who have no love for archaeologists; letters in the April 1982 issue of *Popular Archaeology* from the treasure hunting fraternity have challenged the wisdom of this expenditure on what they see as an obscurantist pastime for an elite group. This is a dangerous state of affairs, especially at a time when we are ruled by a doctrinaire Government dedicated to the ruthless cutting back of state spending and the privatisation of almost every aspect of national administration. In the face of this challenge from what is beginning to style itself 'the alternative archaeology', we cannot afford to ignore our obligation to present the results of our work to the general public. But I will return to this aspect of communication later.

Let me now try to define some of the elements of the system of information flow in archaeology. The starting point must obviously be the archaeological resource itself – that is to say, the vestiges of past societies and environments in Britain in the soil, in the landscape, in artefacts ranging from flint debitage to Gothic cathedrals. These are subjected more or less systematically to survey and recording in a variety of ways. Survey from the air and on the ground reveals landscapes, settlements, and individual monuments which are recorded by plans and drawings, and by written accounts, whilst fieldwalking produces artefactual materials, often in

10

abundance. There is another important source of information – that resulting from archival study, using legal documents such as wills and conveyances, and the great wealth of topographical drawings and paintings, all of which are to be found in public record offices and – decreasingly – in private collections and archieves.

The work of collecting and collating these data began in the 16th century in Britain, though the systematic approach may be said to date from the end of the last century with the institution of the Victoria County History. The work of the three Royal Commissions began in 1908 and the Ordnance Survey index was initiated by O G S Crawford in the 1920s (though the present record owes its form and scope to the vision of Charles Phillips in the years following World War II). The work of listing historic buildings began as early as 1932, although it was the great Town and Country Planning Act of 1947 that set up the present system. And in the past decade we have seen the establishment of sites and monuments records in most counties in England and in the four Welsh archaeological trust regions.

Excavation is a monstrous producer of data. Once upon a time, when I started excavating over a quarter of a century ago, the product of an excavation was a series of plans and sections and a modest selection of finds – not everything, because we kept only those sherds of coarse pottery that appeared to show something, such as rims and bases, and we were not too keen on small fragments of Roman tile. Nowadays, however, nothing is ever thrown away – intentionally that is, although the treasure hunters take particular pleasure in searching excavation spoil heaps and producing handfuls of coins and brooches. Animal bones, snail shells, beetle shards, seeds, pollen are all collected in great quantities and painstakingly identified and analysed. Samples are taken for phosphate analysis, radiocarbon dating, mortar analysis, archaeomagnetic dating, thermoluminescence, dendrochronology and goodness knows what else. The punctilious and meticulous examination and analysis of the total data yield from latter-day excavation is producing an immeasurably greater understanding of the past than the crude interpretation of a relatively arbitrary selection that was the rule a couple of decades ago. Nevertheless, the total data yield is immense.

A third source of data is represented by the collections in our museums, which are being added to continuously as a result of donations from private collections and chance finds. So much of this material has only recently been subjected to systematic study and cataloguing, and it represents a component of the total archaeological data base that is often overlooked or under-rated.

Before I look at systems of archaeological data handling, let me try to define the ways in which this immense data base needs to be utilized, since this must surely define to a considerable extent the way in which the data need to be organized. Basically, I would identify two main uses of archaeological data. The first is obviously research – that is to say, extending our knowledge of the past – and the second is administrative – by which I mean the identification of those manifestations of past human activity that need to be protected and preserved or which may serve as locations for further research. There is a third use, that of the presentation of the past to laymen through museums and monuments that are open to the public, but this is in many ways a secondary use and I do not propose to pursue it here.

The research function of the archaeological data base is one that is basically internal to the discipline of archaeology. The data can be presented in a variety of ways. They can be site-specific, for example, all the data relating to a single site being accessioned and presented together – essentially the excavation report. Another research use of data is the synthetic report – the corpora dealing with a single class of artefact, for example, or the comparative study of all known examples of a certain type of field monument, be it causewayed camp or Wealden hall house. Then there is the regional study, giving a diachronic account of the archaeology of a given area. Complementary to this is the synchronic study of all that is known about society or some aspect of it across the country at a given period. And, of course, there are many variations and combinations of these basic types of research.

For administrative purposes, the data base is used to locate and quantify all the evidence of past human activity as a function of land-use planning. Thus it is necessary to have accurate details of location, size, and extent of field monuments and buildings, and to be able to assign these to certain chronological and typological categories. Where statutory protection· is provided through Ancient Monuments or Town and Country Planning legislation, this needs to be known, and the state of preservation and completeness is another factor that can be of considerable relevance in decision-making. These decisions can take a number of forms. For example, they may relate to the destruction of the heritage, with or without proper recording. They may also operate positively, as part of a policy for acquisition or for the extension of statutory protection. There is thus a link between this function and the research function: such decisions may be made on the basis of a value judgement, which will be less subjective if the importance or uniqueness of a monument or landscape can be evaluated on the basis of adequate research data.

I hope that my necessarily simplistic analysis of the potential uses of an archaeological data base will serve to illustrate the desiderata of that data base. An immensely wide range of material is encompassed, from the micro scale – as represented by the artefactual and environmental yields of excavation – to the macro scale such as the statutory definition of Conservation Areas in historic towns. Let us now look at practicalities.

It would be utterly Utopian – and, indeed, I would say counterproductive – to envisage all these data going on to one gargantuan mainframe computer somewhere in the depths of Fortress House, to be drawn upon alike by County Planning Oficers, unit finds administrators, PhD students, and amateur field groups, Whilst I am sure the computer specialists will assure me that this would be a modest requirement in computer terms, the problems of ensuring uniformity in the input data, emanating as they inevitably do from a multiplicity of sources, would involve an expenditure out of all proportion to the potential use of this super data-base.

Nevertheless, I do believe very firmly that a central repository of certain classes and levels of data needs to be established, and could indeed be established without excessive expenditure. Some years ago I chaired a working party to study archaeological records at the request of the Royal Commission on Historical Monuments (England). Our report (RCHM(E) 1975) was a somewhat naive document, but I believe that its main recommendation – the establishment of what we called a National Non-Intensive Sites and Monuments Record – was an important one, but one which, alas, has not yet been implemented. It was a very modest proposal – a computer file of sites and monuments covering location, administrative details, a description that encompassed generic type, form, condition, and period on a broad classification, control data, and an optional bibliographical entry. Bearing in mind the developments in computer technology since 1975, when our report was published, I would now be a little more ambitious. For example, it should not present too many difficulties to add data on certain broad artefactual and environmental categories where excavations had taken place, along with radiocarbon and other dates, and a relatively complete bibliography.

The report proposed that the National Non-Intensive Record should be based on a complete coverage of the country by Intensive Records at County or multi-County level. Certain recommendations were made as to the contents of these Records, which it was hoped would be computer-based and compatible both with one another and with the National Non-Intensive Record. I fear that implementation of the 1975 report – if it should ever come about – would be too late for this pious hope to be realized: there seems to be a somewhat bewildering incompatibility between the County SMRs that are already in operation. However, I am sanguine that it would not be impossible to overcome this relatively minor problem.

Now, the question will inevitably be asked: who is going to use this partial data base and how? In its original form, as set out in the report, there was no very satisfactory answer, since I now realize that the content of the proposed National Non-Intensive Record was inadequate for research and was, moreover, duplicated in much more detail at County level so far as potential administrative users were concerned. However, the introduction of more data on excavation yields, dating, and bibliographical material would, in my opinion, make it a very valuable research tool, since it would direct researchers to the detailed excavation archives in a more effective way: the preliminary coarse screening using such a record could potentially be undertaken with a measure of confidence.

That, then, is my central date-base – an effective and relatively inexpensive tool, comprising a comprehensive sites and monuments record with an index to excavation products and a relatively complete bibliography. This would be supported by a network of fuller records at County or regional level, either wholly or partially held on computer. I have reservations about the degree to which such records should be stored on computer. Of course there are no technological reasons why every component of a County sites and monuments record should not be computerized, but there must surely be financial constraints operating against this. Given the frequency with which individual site files are likely to be searched in depth, it would seem to be economically feasible to put no more than the essential indexing elements into the computer file and to retain the full documentation in its original form. However, I should be delighted if someone could satisfactorily demonstrate to me that it is cheaper to put it all on tape or floppy disk than to put the documents into boxes or files!

Material from such records, whether 'Non-Intensive' or 'Intensive', can easily be outputted in a variety of forms. It is a relatively simple operation to select and format material for direct or indirect outputs – that is to say, as conventional printouts or as floppy disks or tapes for reproduction in conventional printed form through phototypesetters or word processors or into microform. Computer graphics should make the production of distribution maps a simple matter. Given an adequate data base at either level, I believe that there is a considerable potential to be realized here in the form of gazetteers and bibliographies that are at the present time produced with great labour and expense, and which are often of rather dubious value.

Let me now turn to the preparation of excavation archives and reports. The micro or mini computer is now becoming as common a piece of equipment for the larger excavation units as a typewriter, a movement pioneered by the DoE Central Excavation Unit. Visitors to units are becoming wearily resigned to the obligatory demonstration of the new tool and what it can do. I must confess to a certain scepticism about the uses to which some of these installations are being put. The time has probably come for a pause for reflection by those working in units as to the purposes for which they are amassing so many data and, more importantly, to what extent it is the responsibility of the excavator to subject these data to increasingly sophisticated statistical analysis. This is, in my view, especially true of work on pottery. With the advent of quantitative studies and the importance now being assigned to fabric analysis, the operations carried out on the immense pottery yield from urban excavations in particular are bulking disproportionately large in post-excavation work. The data are all painstakingly entered into the computer file and juggled around with, but the results are for the most part disappointingly slight – some enormous mountains are giving birth to a very few, pathetically ridiculous mice. To mix my metaphors, the result is a classic example of overkill. Given that it is now accepted policy to retain all material from excavations indefinitely for future research, I would strongly recommend that a careful re-assessment should be carried out of the procedures for examining most of the artefactual material – and also, indeed, of the environmental material – arising from excavations and for recording them. The computer is in some ways a dangerous tool, since the availability of a rapid method of analysis of data is paradoxically proving to be a potential source of delay in the overall processing time, with negligible increase in research information yield.

Other aspects of the data yield from excavations, such as details of structures and other features, can greatly benefit from the availability of computer storage and analysis. Barry Cunliffe's work in analysing the thousands of pits and postholes at Danebury has been facilitated and enriched by computer analysis, and it cannot be claimed that the processing time was extended, since most of the examination and recording of these features – apart from certain aspects of analysis of deposits for environmental data – was carried out in the field during the course of the excavation proper and not during the post-excavation period. Work by the Central Excavation Unit – at Winklebury, for example – has similarly demonstrated the worth of computer handling of such data. It could well be that artefactual material could similarly benefit from computer analysis if the data recording were to run concurrently with the excavation, but this would probably be impracticable on urban Roman and medieval excavations, or possible only if the personnel were greatly augmented, which is unlikely in present conditions.

For maximum utility, computer files must be compiled on site during excavations, all data, both artefactual and structural, being analysed and fed through a remote terminal into the data-base or into an on-site microcomputer. This technique was pioneered in the USA; it was first successfully introduced into this country by Ian Graham and more recently adopted by the Central Excavation Unit. It is an admirable innovation and one that should be encouraged; however, there are a number of safeguards that must accompany its introduction.

First and foremost, it requires careful and adequate preparation. Too many archaeologists are still illiterate so far as computers are concerned and it is all too easy to compile a computer file from which it is impossible to retrieve data in any meaningful form. This state of affairs is changing, and the availability of progressively cheaper personal computers should mean that the new generation of archaeologists will be able to use computers as deftly and effectively as they now wield trowels or ballpoints. Of course, this is slow to percolate backwards into the universities: a study of the syallabuses for archaeological degrees at British universities reveals a distressing lack of appropriate courses for undergraduates.

Another problem that will need to be overcome is that of compatibility of systems. I sometimes think that archaeologists are the only remaining individualists left in British society; standardisation often seems to be a dirty word. Everyone has to work out his own recording system from first principles, and the result is that there is a bewildering diversity in documentation and cataloguing. For non-automatic data recording systems this is no more than a irritant, but it can be a serious handicap as soon as computerized systems are involved. I can think of three occasions in the past year when I have been told by the proud possessors of a new mini or micro-computer that they have not adopted the CEU system but have worked out one of their own which is superior in some esoteric way. This may permit them to indulge in some new and exciting form of number-crunching, but is it really in the best interests of research? For comparative studies – and that, surely, is what archaeology is all about – it must be more efficacious to be able to work directly with a number of data files from different sources without having to waste time in carrying out elaborate exercises to ensure compatibility of outputs. This is perhaps of lesser importance between individual excavations when the general information content is being studied, but for more specialized studies on, say, pottery, brooches, or snail shells, compatibility seems to me to be essential. If nothing else comes out of this conference I would hope that some progress might be made towards the establishment of viable standards of compatibility.

Let me turn now to the various forms of output required from the different data-bases to ensure that efficient mutual comprehension which is implicit in the title of my lecture. Right at the beginning, I would like to state my position without equivocation: the traditional methods of publication are no longer cost-effective or viable for the majority of archaeological reporting. A handsome thick book – a Society of Antiquaries Research Report, for example – full of drawings and plans and tables and catalogues and plates is a grand thing to heft in one's hand and to contemplate on one's shelves, but it is a dinosaur, a survival from those prehistoric times of twenty-five years ago when rescue archaeology had never been heard of and cluster analysis was an arcane concern of the scientist. As I have already stressed, the total data product from a contemporary excavation is too colossal to permit it to be contained within the covers of a single volume. What is more, no one really wants or needs his own archive of every major excavation. The old-fashioned excavation report is a compendium of several distinct types of information product and it is difficult to conceive of any archaeological polymath today who would have the scholarly apparatus to comprehend and digest the totality. The result is that attempts to bring all the available data together in one publication are less and less saleable — a point which as a publisher I have close to my heart – and so the results are becoming available to fewer and fewer people.

Let us look at a typical traditional excavation report. It will usually start with a meticulous account of the excavation, feature by feature, layer by layer – a great indigestible expanse of unreadable text guaranteed to send the most assiduous seeker after truth to sleep within a short time. This will be illustrated by a wealth of drawings – sections and plans by the score, many of them large and awkward to handle and to consult while reading the book. This is usually followed by a long section on interpretation, related to the preceding excavation description and to the following inventories of finds and specialist reports. For most readers, this is likely to be the only section that is read attentively and to some purpose.

The inventories and specialist reports remain unread in most cases, I suspect, by all except fellow specialists. For most readers – and by this I mean archaeologists and not laymen – the interpretation of the site by the excavator is in general accepted at its face value, so long as it is well founded and supported by relevant key data. I wonder how many of us here today have ever carried out the operation, so zealously set forth by those who cannot bear to see the traditional excavation report disappear, of checking every statement made in an interpretation section against the relevant descriptions in the excavation section and the catalogue entries? I have possibly done so two or three times, where a site being reported that was directly comparable with one that I was excavating and where the excavator's interpretation was at variance with my own theories. I may add that on no occasion was I able, on the basis of the data presented, to construct an irrefutable case for rejecting the excavator's own interpretation: this is attributable, without doubt, to the fact that recording is not an objective process, and any apparently factual account of an excavation is in fact highly subjective, the data recorded being consciously or subconsciously passed through the observer's own interpretative filter. We must never forget that excavation is not in any strict sense a scientific action, if only because replication is by definition impossible: as Wheeler never failed to remind us, 'archaeology is destruction'.

The myth – for myth it is – that it is possible to reconstruct an excavation from a detailed research report was very effectively exploded by Leslie Alcock (1977-8) in a brilliant paper on archaeological publication. As he points out, referring to the classic reinterpretations of the Cranborne Chase settlements (Hawkes 1947, 36-78) and of the mortuary enclosure under Wor Barrow (Piggott 1954, 57-60), 'it is a matter of historical fact that such re-interpretations, based not on re-excavation, but simply on a reconsideration of the published evidence, have not multiplied in print since Hawkes and Piggott demonstrated the possibility; and it is a matter of comment that these classic re-interpretations are of very simple structures. There is no range of clinical experience to show, for instance, that it is possible to re-interpret a complex stratificaion.'

The inventories of finds and the specialist reports are, of course, the province of the specialists. Those interested in coarse pottery or flints or slag analysis are generally little concerned with the sites from which the raw materials of their specialist studies are derived. Here I would exempt from my strictures those carrying out environmental studies: few of them, if any, are interested in fossil pollens or snails shells for their own sake. However, as scientists they often display a tendency to write for other scientists rather than archaeologists, and their contributions are sometimes difficult for the latter to comprehend adequately; it often follows that the scientists' finds are not properly or accurately integrated into the synthesis section of the main report.

What, then, does the traditional excavation report comprise, and for whom are the various components primarily of value? The core of any report is the interpretation or synthesis section, which is likely to be read by the largest number of archaeologists. This number might well be larger, and the readership might extend outside the conventional professional core, if there were not an obligation with the conventional format for a purchaser to pay for a good deal of expensively printed material that is of no interest to him, and which he would never read. Then there is the description of the excavation – unread in most cases by all but a few of those who buy or borrow the report, and included to justify the interpretation. Finally there are the specialist sections, read only by fellow specialists, which may be as many as 150 in the case of Romano-British coarse pottery and less than ten in the case of iron-slag analyses. There is surely a case for a thorough-going rethink of the modes of communicating these differing sets of data to their repsective audiences. The Frere report (DoE 1975) proposed four levels of record. For Level III, it recommended 'publication in journal or occasional papers as required, or available as duplicates, microfiche, microfilm, or computer print-out' and for Level IV the somewhat gnomic 'publication in multiple copies'. I believe that these two levels had little relevance in 1975, and that they are meaningless in contemporary terms; what is needed is a conflation of the two as a package or as individual elements.

The 'synthesized description: with supporting data' represent to some extent the interpretation or discussion sections of traditional reports and, as I have indicated already, I believe that these would command relatively large readerships in conventional printed form, thereby increasing communication above the present level, having regard to the financial constraints that apply to traditional reports.

The Level III material – the 'full illustration and description of all structural and stratigraphical relationships' and 'classified find-lists and find drawings, and all specialist analyses' – should in my view no longer be available in printed form – as journal publications or occasional papers, according to the Frere report – but only in microform and also, where appropriate, as computer files, accessible as print-outs or other forms of computer outputs such as disks.

In this way the different readerships whose requirements are currently ill served by the traditional excavation report would be enabled to acquire just the package they want, with no extraneous material or additional expense. The 'generalist' – whether archaeologist or lay reader – could acquire the printed synthesis and the specialist just those items that related to his or her specific concern, the latter in the form of microfiche, disk, print-out etc. For the library it would be possible to buy the printed volume and the complete microform package (including the structural and stratigraphical relationships), whilst archaeological units could chose between microform or computer reports. In this way it should be possible to adapt the report material to specific users, according to their precise needs and to their storage and retrieval capabilities.

It would be absurd if all the raw data put into computer files in the field had to be reworked completely before they could be made available as the non-printed elements of the package that I have just described. This is another reason why the time for reassessment is ripe, if not overdue. Not only should there be greater compatibility of systems for inputting and analysis, but there should also be agreed standard systems for producing outputs for dissemination. Communication would be that much more effective if we all spoke the same language, if not necessarily the same dialect. This should be the main thrust of research into the applications of information technology in archaeology in the immediate future. If we can get this right and get general acceptance of the systems proposed, it should be a relatively simple task to fit them into other systems – the MDA system for museums collections, for example, or the national and regional sites and monuments record that I was advocating earlier. The existence of such an interlocking network of archaeological data will form the foundation upon which a great deal of fundamental research could be based, enabling spatial, chronological, and typological relationships to be identified and studied with much greater ease and confidence than is the case at the present time. And there is no reason why this should result in a massive increase in expenditure: hardware is already being installed at a growing rate, and access to equipment is much easier in universities and local authorities. So long as archaeologists do not get misled by the computer, by what a French colleague once described to me as 'folies d'ordinateur', the information yield will be greater and better marshalled and the research potential greatly increased.

I have been dealing so far with communication between archaeologists, but I referred at the beginning of the paper to our obligation to communicate the results of our work to the public. This is one area where man still has an edge over machines. Indirectly, however, the application of new technology and the development of new and improved systems should contribute to improving communication between archaeologists and the public. In recent years archaeologists have been so overwhelmed by the task of recording and analysing the massive data product of excavations and survey that they have paid less and less heed to the obligation to interpret and synthesize these data: I am sure we can all cite examples of excavation reports which are 99% record and 1% interpretation. Better data handling systems will free them from much of the bondage that has hitherto been imposed upon them by the weight of data, a new approach to publication will encourage interpretation and synthesis, which could well be sounder as a result of the more reliable data processing, and there could well be more time and greater incentives for the communication of these results to a wider public in the various forms of media. Perhaps I am being a little idealistic, but I would remind you that there is a strong element of realism underlying what I am advocating. 'Only connect' must be our watchword not only in relation to our colleagues but also to the public at large – we neglect the latter at our peril.

References

Alcock, L, 1977-8 Excavation and publication: some comments, *Proc Soc Antiq Scotland*, 109, 1-6

DoE, 1975 *Principles of publication in rescue archaeology*

Hawkes, C F C, 1947 Britons, Romans and Saxons round Salisbury and in Cranborne Chase, *Archaeol J*, 104, 27–81

Piggott, S, 1954 *Neolithic cultures of the British Isles*

RCHM(E), 1975 *Report of the Working Party on Archaeological Records*, Royal Commission on Historical Monuments (England)

CHAPTER 2

A BRIEF INTRODUCTION TO THE TECHNOLOGY OF 'IT'

J. D. Wilcock
Research Centre for Computer Archaeology
North Staffordshire Polytechnic

1982 has been chosen by the British government to publicise information technology (IT), the acquisition, processing, storage and dissemination of vocal, pictorial, textual and numeric information using a combination of computing and telecommunications. Many of these techniques are not new, but the combination of them has been made possible by the increased availability of the microchip. From 1982 to 1984 is only two years, so it behoves us to wonder whether Orwell's "Big Brother is watching you" might be a technical possibility, and the disturbing truth is yes, if we do not keep control of the proliferating computerised data-banks of personal information and the interlinking of computer systems by communications networks.

"Computer" is an emotive word to many. Some think computers are frightening, but this is fear of the unknown. Others think they are annoying and make silly errors (such as the million pound gas bill and similar anecdotes related by the popular press), but these errors are chiefly human errors in programming or data magnified by the computer – "garbage in, garbage out". The "electronic brain" image is a familiar misconception; computers cannot think, nor do they remotely approach the complexity of the human brain. Computers are impersonal, and affect services, removing the human touch and making redundant low-level clerical jobs. To their acolytes they are fascinating, even addictive. But the most responsible attitude to take towards computers should be that they are useful, modern tools of the Space Age. They can be regarded as unintelligent information systems clerks, obedient, accurate, tireless and speedy, with an exceptionally good memory. Contrary to the public conception that they are solely mathematical calculating machines, their chief uses are the recording and retrieval of information, and data can be represented not just numerically but also with alphabetic characters and pictorially (computer graphics).

Modern uses of the computer are legion. Supermarkets are beginning to use bar codes to identify packages at the checkout; the computer, in addition to supplying the prices and adding up the bills, decrements the stock record, sends orders to the automated warehouses to bring out more goods, institutes the reorder process, keeps records of takings, and communicates with the Head Office. Government is a very big user of computers, travel agents use computer terminals to interrogate hotel, airline, ferry and package tour records, and to make bookings. Building Societies, banks and the Post Office use computers widely in the services they provide. County and Borough Councils handle planning, rates demands, educational records, salaries and word processing by computer. Hospitals use computers in analytical laboratories, and some hospitals computerise all their admissions, out-patient, patient, appointment and ward records; 'expert systems', i.e. data-bases constructed by experts, in this case doctors and specialists, are even used for diagnosis, and for training new doctors. Libraries are beginning to use computers for their cataloguing, indexing and issuing, with bar codes in books and on reader cards. Finally, many computers are used to control transport systems: railways, air traffic control, the planning and design of roads as well as the control of traffic and distribution fleets. All these applications in the High Street involve the processing of information, and numerical data play a comparatively small part. Clearly computers influence most aspects of our lives now.

The History of the Development of Computers and Microelectronics

Computers have been around for longer than most people realise. The first mechanical calculating machines were invented by Pascal and Leibniz in the seventeenth century. These machines, which used toothed wheels and calculated in decimal, were the basis of the "hand-churning" type of calculator still in use until the 1960s.

The real father of the computer was Charles Babbage, who was interested in many aspects of science and technology. Mathematical tables were known to be inaccurate in those days, firstly because they were calculated by teams of humans, and secondly because printers introduced typographical errors. Babbage set out to remove both sources of error in the tables by calculating them by machine, and by automatically setting the type. His "Difference Engine" achieved this, and was capable of evaluating any polynomial. Babbage's next idea was to design a machine which would be capable of performing not just one job, like the Difference Engine, but any job by programming it with a series of instructions. He called this the "Analytical Engine" (1820). It used columns of toothed wheels to store 10,000 numbers to 50 places of decimals; it had what we would call an Arithmetic Unit (the "Mill"), which could perform additions, subtractions, multiplications and divisions; it could input numbers from switched wheels, and output was by reading the positions of wheels. Programming was by punched cards derived from the Jacquard loom – and punched cards are still used in some computer installations today. Babbage's assistant, the first computer programmer, was Ada Augusta Lovelace, daughter of Lord Byron the poet. She was, unusually for a woman in those days, a Cambridge mathematician with a First Class degree. She wrote many treatises on the capabilities of the Analytical Engine, and in the end probably understood the potential of the machine, the first true computer, better than Babbage did himself.

If the first computer appeared in 1820, then why have computers really come to the fore only comparatively recently? Firstly, in 1820 there was no real need for computers; secondly, there was little money for their development; and thirdly there was no machine tool industry to support their manufacture – all the toothed wheels had to be made by craftsmen. Development came when these three conditions were satisfied, in the Second World War; there was an absolute need for computers, for the side with the best computers was going to win the war; there was plenty of money available for defence; and there was a machine tool industry. The first working computer, the COLOSSUS, was used at Bletchley Park to crack German codes; and in the USA a computer was used to design the atomic bomb. The Automatic Sequence Controlled Calculator (ASCC) in the USA was a mechanical machine based on Babbage's ideas, but by the 1940s electronic valves had been developed, and these were used in the First Generation electronic computers. In the 1950s the Second Generation computers were based on Shockley's transistor and other semiconductor components. From the transistor, one component on a semiconductor chip, developed Small Scale Integration (SSI), 10 components/chip by 1960, Medium Scale Integration (MSI), 100 components/chip by 1965, Large Scale Integration (LSI), 1000 components/chip by 1970, and Very Large Scale Integration (VLSI), 10000 components/chip by 1975. LSI was used in the Third Generation computers.

But increasing complexity of circuitry on a chip was leading to increased cost to the customer – not that the circuits cost more to manufacture, but that the market for the more complex circuits was less, and the development costs had to be recouped over a smaller number of items (a larger unit cost). The electronic engineers got themselves out of this quandary by inventing the MICROPROCESSOR, a general purpose control circuit which can be programmed to perform a large variety of tasks. The microprocessor, in addition to being the basis of many control units in domestic and industrial products, has made cheap computing power (the MICROCOMPUTER) readily available. Moreover, the sale of millions of microprocessors has caused the cost to come tumbling down. Examples of new types of product made available by the microprocessor are word processors, facsimile mail transmitters, miniaturised TV sets, microcomputers, TV games, hand calculators, electronic musical instruments, electronic toys, cost meters for telephones, pocket digital thermometers, vending machines, and robots.

The "Microprocessor Revolution" is not wholly a revolution in manufacturing techniques – in any case the development of SSI, MSI, LSI and VLSI from the transistor has been a continuous process. The true revolution has been the increased availability of computing power. A microprocessor costs only a few Pounds Sterling – certainly one can buy a powerful computer now for less than the cost of a new car. Microprocessors will be used in the home without thinking, for a variety of uses, for example as hand calculators, liquid crystal display watches, timers, cooker controllers, washing machine controllers, and communications controllers (TV set, telephone, recorders, etc.) and they will form a necessary part of car controls in the future.

Videotex

VIDEOTEX is the international name for the system of information transmission which uses a modified TV set to display "pages" of text and low-resolution graphics. Videotex may be divided into two main modes of operation, TELETEXT and VIEWDATA.

Teletext is the simpler of the two modes, and is broadcast via television transmitters by the BBC as CEEFAX (See Facts) and by the IBA as ORACLE. Since there is no possibility of two-way interaction, any viewer must be able to access any page within a reasonable time; in practice this restricts the total number of pages to about 100, and they are transmitted in a continuous loop or "round robin". Thus Teletext is limited to mass market information, such as news headlines, sports results, the weather forecast, TV programmes, travel blackspots and consumer information.

Viewdata is transmitted by British Telecom as PRESTEL. The transmission channel is by telephone, to and from a central computer. Full two-way interaction is available, so several million pages may be provided. A "tree" method of access is used, the required page being selected either by a known code obtained from a directory, or by the user steering himself through the system via general indexes (the "trunk" of the tree), and specialised indexes ("branches") to the page required ("twig"). Each information page, excluding indexes, is charged via the telephone account, and there are also connection charges plus a normal telephone bill, so the system is expensive and consequently less used than BT and its predecessor The Post Office had hoped.

The low resolution graphics of Videotex are made up of "pixels", small blocks each occupying the space of one text character and made up of six smaller blocks, 3 vertical by 2 horizontal, each small block being ON (grey or white) or OFF (black). Thus fairly crude graphic diagrams can be built up, such as large blocked titles, and colour combinations are also possible.

There are a few special features of Videotex which should be mentioned. A "response frame", necessarily restricted to Viewdata, allows the user to supply textual information in reply, such as name, address, credit card number, orders or bookings. An extended version of this allows free text to be sent to other users via the central computer, a facility called "electronic mail". Finally, computer programs may also be sent as "telesoftware" pages. Under development are higher resolution pictures (of the quality of photographs, and probably in as many as 256 hues), such as experimental "Picture Prestel", which could make the transmission of photographs possible. One very important current development is the Prestel Gateway, by which third party computers can be accessed without any limitations of Prestel itself. This will help to establish a wide audience of data-base users, by making numerous data-bases available through ordinary telephone and television receivers.

The Home/School/Office Information Centre of the Future

It is likely that the TV set in the corner of our home will be replaced by an information centre comprising TV screen, full keyboard, telephone, microprocessor, backing memory, videotape or videodisc, hard copy printer and probably a camera. This will make available the following facilities:

1. Television
2. Videotex
3. Video recorder for TV programmes, with playback for recordings and bought-out films. Videodiscs may be an alternative.
4. Teach-yourself facility (using recorded Viewdata pages or bought-out Computer Aided Learning (CAL) packages)
5. Terminal to remote main frame computer
6. Stand-alone microcomputer with telesoftware
7. Telephone/Videophone/Teleconferencing/Facsimile transmission for documents
8. Electronic mail receiver/transmitter
9. Word Processor (typing and editing of text on the screen, with formatting and hard copy)
10. Response frames and remote ordering
11. Financial transactions
12. Network station to Local Area Network (LAN), optical fibre networks or cable TV

Such terminals will make possible office work from the home, and prototypes are already available.

Videotapes

Manufacturers have not yet standardised on systems, and there are three main types in use:

1. VHS (Baird, Ferguson, DER, Granada), with 3 hour tapes
2. Beta System (Sony), 3 hr 15min, slightly smaller tapes

3. Philips V2000 (Philips, Grundig), 8 hr, larger tapes.

A good system can be expected to offer remote timers, which will record a TV programme in the absence of the operator, or record one programme while the user is watching another; fast picture search; speeded-up or slow-motion replays; freeze-frame and remote control.

Videodiscs

Again there are three types:

1. *Capacitance Electronic Disc* (CED) (RCA)
    Pits are disposed on both sides of a groove tracked by a stylus. This is really a high-precision gramophone record, and is the cheapest of the three methods, but there is no freeze-frame, no random access, and the stylus and disc wear out. The medium is only suitable for continuously-run films.
2. *Laser Vision Disc* (Phillips)
    A metallic layer embedded in clear plastic has pits which are detected by a low-powered laser beam. There is no physical contact, and therefore no wear.
3. *Video High Density* (VHD) (Thorn-EMI, Ferguson)
    This uses an electronic capacitance sensing device, and the tracking is electronic. There are timing tracks on both sides of a central information track. Two sound tracks are available, for stereo or for two languages.

The systems, except CED, are capable of fast and random access picture search, speeded-up and backwards replay, slow-motion, freeze-frame and remote control. The laser or VHD types are capable of storing and retrieving a large number of single frames, and an archaeological application of this would be photos of excavation or museum artefacts, with pages of text as on microfilm; the capacity of one disc is considerably greater than a microfilm or fiche.

Winchester Discs

'Winchester' discs are totally-enclosed magnetic discs which offer several Megabytes of storage for a microcomputer. These are a larger and more reliable means of providing backing store than the ubiquitous floppy disc, but are rather expensive, and some form of backup must also be provided (a video recorder is a cheap solution for this).

Word Processing

'Word processing' is the production of text by electronic means. A Word Processor is a microcomputer with video screen, keyboard, backing store (cassette, floppy disc, or hard disc), and a high-quality printer. Facilities are the capture and recording of text, with editing on screen (correction, insertion and deletion of characters, words, sentences and paragraphs), and formatting for output (e.g. right justification, centering, tabulation). Many other facilities are possible, e.g. an arithmetic facility for adding up colums of figures in the text, information retrieval for obtaining data to be included in the text, automatic page numbering, automatic headings and footings. Extra hardware may provide multiple screens, microfilm output, electronic mail, or a 'filmsetter' (which can produce multi-font letterpress-like type images on photographic paper, a facility used now by many newspapers and publishing houses). A typical high-quality printer is the Daisy-Wheel Printer, which has a print or 'daisy wheel' with typefaces on the 'petals'. Fonts may easily be changed by replacing the daisy wheel.

Networks

Computers are now linked by networks, either locally (the Local Area Network or LAN), nationally by leased lines, coaxial cables or optical fibres, or internationally by satellites.

The Local Area Network has two main forms: the Cambridge Ring, around which 'packets' of information circulate; and the Ethernet, which is linear with a complex system of checking for collisions between packets and subsequent retransmission.

Cable systems could possibly carry up to 30 channels of information in future TV networks, leading to a much wider choice of viewing, and possibly to the eventual end of fixed-time transmissions.

Telephone exchanges are also becoming computerised (e.g. BT System X) with short-code calling, call diversion to another number, reminder calls, repeat calls to engaged numbers, holding one call while speaking to another, 3-way calls, charge recording and advice, call barring, repeat last call, and recording the sources of all calls.

Data Capture Methods
Data capture methods are also increasing in type and diversity:

1. Keyboard – will be with us for a while yet, but increasingly versatile, with cursor control, and software function keys
2. Voice capture – voice recognition and understanding is developing, but efficient systems which work for many users in other than laboratory conditions will be a while yet
3. Tones – can be used to transmit digits, and robots also use them to communicate with each other and with humans
4. Handwritten characters – can be recognised by computer using a tablet or 'datapad'
5. Magnetic ink character recognition – used for digits
6. Optical character recognition – bar codes can provide numerical

information, while special fonts (e.g. OCRA) can be recognised directly

7.   Tablet with stylus – detection of position of stylus can be used to capture maps, plans and artefact drawings, and also to select items from a 'menu' of software routines

8.   TV camera – can be used to capture artefact shapes and profiles, and software can then enhance contrast, window (i.e. clip) the picture, calculate the centre line, rotate and normalise the picture, and calculate profile codes for similarity studies

9.   Menus – selected by stylus on a tablet, touch pads on a screen, or light pen on a screen.

Microfilm

Microfilm is increasingly being used as an acceptable alternative for the publication or archaeological archive information, such as the Level 3 data for a large site, or for mixed-media publication. Computers may also produce text and diagrammatic information directly on microfilm. The microfilm may be roll film, film jackets, film folios, microfiche or aperture cards. More and more archaeological publications are appearing on microfiche, which is very cheap to produce and post, but of course requires access to a microfiche reader.

Types of Microcomputer

For the information of archaeologists bemused by the rapid development of microcomputers the following brief summary is offered:

1.   Hobby microcomputers – these require some technical knowledge and are bought as do-it-yourself kits or single printed circuit boards with no frills of any sort. They have a small memory, and often use cassettes as backing store. Most have BASIC in read only memory (ROM), but some only use machine code and have operating systems with cryptic commands.

2.   Developed games – these are a spin-off from TV games and electronic amusement arcade games. Some allow plug-in cassettes or ROMs for more games.

3.   'Domestic Appliance' microcomputers – these are designed to be sold, taken home, plugged in and used by persons with no special technical knowledge, just like any other domestic appliance. They are compact, usually in a single box. They are not particularly expandable, and some use their own incompatible peripherals, without which they will not work. The more expensive ones usually have floppy discs and a printer.

4.   'Building Block' microcomputers – these have several different units connected by cables. To upgrade the sytem new or additional units are added, e.g. more store, floppy discs, Winchester discs, printers, tablets, displays, network interface, etc.

It is only the fourth category of microcomputer which should be considered for archaeological use. Archaeological systems require a lot of data, and thus both memory and backing memory (cassettes, floppy discs, or Winchester disc) must be large and fast. The speed and type of microprocessor is less important, although British computer archaeologists are currently recommending standardisation on 8-bit Z80-based machines, with programs written in PASCAL or BASIC. However, the situation is changing weekly, and no doubt in due course 16-bit machines will be a better proposition. A high-quality printer is essential if any type or word processing is contemplated, and these are expensive. The price of the electronic part of the hardware is in general falling, but the peripheral devices, being electromechanical and requiring frequent servicing, are generally increasing in price. A service contract will cost 10% – 15% of the capital cost of the hardware, annually. Furthermore, the cost of software bought from the manufacturer is now approaching 50% of the total cost, and licensing agreements are becoming increasingly strict, for example a program being licensed to be run on one machine only. Finally, media costs (printer paper, floppy discs, etc.) can amount to a significant sum each year. Perhaps the best advice to give is to consult other computer archaeologists and see what they recommend in the way of hardware, and particularly if they have any working software systems which they have written themselves and are willing to make available.

Summary

What use can be made of the new Information Science in archaeology? Some ideas are:

> Data-bases and data-banks
> Videodiscs of excavation and museum artefacts
> Microfiche of publications, maps, colour photographs
> Person-to-person teleconferencing
> Electronic mail
> Word processing for publication
> Facsimile transmission of documents
> Transmission of photographic images by Picture PRESTEL

Perhaps one day it may even be possible to reconstruct an artefact in three dimensional form, using a hologram derived from a high resolution interference pattern received from facsimile transmission, or from video-disc, using laser light.

A more general remark is that at present it is more efficient to use computers to produce indexes to drawings, maps, photographs and other media, rather than actually to store graphical information on the computer.

What changes, if any, in archaeological methodology will have to be made to take advantage of the new techniques?
A few thoughts are:

Microcomputers and recorders on site
Increased discipline in the use of information retrieval and storage methods
Appreciation of the proper uses of statistics
Increased use of computer graphics

Is this a case of the Information Technology tail wagging the Archaeology dog, or are the new techniques so important that Archaeology must comply?

CHAPTER 3

SETTING UP AN ARCHAEOLOGICAL COMPUTER SYSTEM – AN INTRODUCTION

Kevin Flude

Museum of London

Introduction

This paper gives a brief introduction to some of the requirements of a viable archaeological computer system. The major problem besetting the archaeological user is computer technology which has advanced so quickly, that it has left those educated in the pre-micro chip era with only a vague idea of what computers can do, and perhaps even less idea of how they do it. This is a problem that is being tackled in schools, university and (by the BBC among others) at home. But for an archaeological organisation wishing to enter the computer age it is a major hurdle to be overcome. Nor is it by any means only a problem for those without first hand experience of computers, as the computer field presents a bewildering and ever changing choice usually couched in technological jargon.

The key to success in the computer world is firstly to buy the right computer for your needs, and secondly to employ or train the right personnel to program and/or run the system. Neither is easy to do. The right computer is one which is big enough to deal with the amount of data and the use to which you eventually decide to put it. It is therefore essential to have an idea of how many people will want to use the machine and how much data they will want to put in it. The right person/s to run the computer may or may not be trained computer staff, but one must weigh up the cost and dangers of the "teach yourself" approach, against the cost benefits in having an archaeologist who understands the problems. It may be that even a relatively inefficient teach yourself approach may, in the long term, be cost effective as a method of promoting computer literacy.

Uses of Computers in Archaeology

It is impossible in an article of this size to describe fully the uses of computers in archaeology. However if one thinks of the computer as an incredibly flexible filing cabinet one can begin to envisage most uses. Indexes and catalogues can be kept and then recordered virtually in any way you please. Information can be packaged to the requirements of enquirers be they academic, public, or from the media, from any part of the data-base held in the computer. As the information recorded can be numeric or easily transformed into numeric information it is relatively easy to undertake statistical work. A graphics facility in the computer allows images to be used as data and provide distribution maps, composite plans, maps, graphs, and drawings to illustrate data and the statistics derived from them. Word processing enormously aids the writing of reports and articles, and the way the organisation can conduct communications both internally and externally.

The computer can be used to record in a compatible form all archaeological work. It can help the director supervise and interpret a site, can be used to produce the report with full cross-referencing, can produce the graphs and plans for the Level Three reports.

Once the information is in the computer it provides the basis for an easily updateable archive. This is particularly important as a computerised archaeological site report can be used for comparison with other sites directly, without further overheads in the form of data collection. Time spent filling in cards and collecting data is reduced. More time can therefore be spent on analysis and checking the validity of conclusions, and one would hope that more synthetic projects would result. This increased ability to assimilate data should enable the more efficient planning of future archaeological projects.

Systems Analysis

The first stage in an investigation of the use of the computer is to undertake a rigorous investigation of the workings of the organisation. This should be carried out without reference to the perceived future role of the computer, or of the practicality of purchasing computer equipment of the required power. There are two reasons for this. The first is that such an investigation pays dividends in allowing rationalisation of procedures and will very probably show unsuspected uses for the computer. Secondly it is important to plan for the future in purchasing computer equipment. It is important to buy equipment that not only deals with the problem in hand but which can at a later stage be augmented to allow expansion into other applications.

The analysis should take the form of a report which outlines work procedures, divides them up into their component parts, person–hours taken in their fulfilment, forms and manuals used, and most importantly the amount of data collected. This can be calculated roughly by taking a random sample (say one hundred of each recording form used) and counting the number of characters used to record the data. This will only be a rough estimate of memory needed by the computer, as it will not take into account any coding used, or computer memory space used up by programs and operation system. At this stage the data are divided into their component parts. For example one might reasonably divide the excavation recording into finds, environmental and field recording. The finds recording could be further divided into pottery and small finds recording. Further division of small finds recording into the following categories could be made: object-name, material, form, description, dimensions, decorations, etc. These could be further sub-divided. The point of this is to decide on the tasks the computer must do, and to give the programmer an idea of what programs to write and the structure of the data with which the programs have to deal.

An attempt to decide the relationship between the components should be made. You may decide that the finds work will be mostly done independently of the excavation recording but that facilities must be available to allow inter-action between the two sections. A decision may be made, for example in the small finds program, that for each type of material recorded there will be many object names associated (Iron:- knife dagger nail etc.), and that each object could be associated with more than one material (knife: iron blade with bone handle etc.).

These facts are important as they will greatly aid the work of the computer programmer. For example if particular items are often referred to together it is important to program in such a way that the two items are easily produced together. If items are rarely used together the programmer will make little effort to facilitate their joint use.

Archaeologists are in a good position for this analysis as they tend to be very aware of their recording systems, but there is a need in computing to go beyond the normally fairly subjective approach, to one where all assumptions are made explicit. Often the side effects of these studies are surprising and useful.

Having finished this analysis flick through copies of *Computer Applications in Archaeology, Science in Archaeology* and MDA Occasional Paper 4 – *Micro Computers in Archaeology*. Leaf through a few micro-computer magazines to get the feel of the jargon and see the type of equipment available. Then embark on a series of visits to those using computers in archaeology. Try to visit a computer show and in particular look at the data collection devices and graphics facilities.

Which Machine?

Having carried out this exercise you are now in a position to consult a computer expert on what type of computer to use. However, you will also be faced with a limited budget and will not in all probability be able to do everything you want to do. You must now either expand your budget, beg borrow or steal computing equipment or adopt a strategy to computerise only that part of the work which the computer could comfortably handle. That is to say a step by step approach is made to the purchase of computer equipment – work out priority projects and buy the equipment necessary to deal with these first.

A Brief Introduction to the Various Machines

Computers can be categorised in a number of ways. Performance is, however, the major determinant. A convenient division can be made between micros, minis and mainframe computers. The boundaries between these are always changing (in the favour of the consumer) so that today's micro–computer is as powerful as yesterday's mainframe. One definition which will serve (but is not strictly accurate) is that micro–computers are best suited to use by one person, minis by several people and mainframes by lots of people at a time. Speed of computing also increases with the size of the computer. As far as cost is concerned one might expect to pay £2000 for a micro–computer system, £20,000 for a mini–computer and hundreds of thousands (to millions) for a mainframe. The sort of organisations for which the various types of computers are designed can be judged from the above costs.

Archaeology deals with a large amount of data mostly in the form of text. The amount of information collected by staff is unusually large in comparison with business or academic organisations. Having only a part of the organisation's data on the computer at any given time does limit the convenience of the computer data–base. I believe that the work of many archaeological organisations warrants the use of a mini–computer. Unfortuantely archaeological budgets are such that a micro–computer system is the most likley to be bought. It is for reasons of a limited capital equipment budget that I stress the need to purchase a computer with a view to later expansion.

The performance of a computer can be defined in the following terms: speed of operation; amount of memory available for immediate use by the computer; amount of data that can be stored and is easily accessible by the computer; and the number of users the computer can support without significantly degrading its performance.

The Central Processor of a computer (CPU) can be judged by the amount of memory that it can hold, and make immediately available for analytical work. This is measured in units of 1000 bytes (one byte is roughly one character of information – a letter such as "a" or "B", a number such as "3" or a symbol, "="). 1000 bytes is called 1K (or kilobyte), so a computer with a 64K CPU can contain 64,000 characters of information in its memory at once. This is approximately 10,000 words of text (although it does not mean that all 64K is available for the user). Data, programs and computer languages also compete for that data space. This article, for example, is aproximately 40K and is about 6,500 words long. You can now see the reason for collecting information on the amount of data to be handled by programs and the need to divide the programming task into sections which can be handled at one go by the computer.

The CPU has 2 forms of memory. Read Only Memory or ROM, which the user is not permitted to change, and RAM (Random Access Memory), which can be both read and written to. Random Access Memory contains programs and data written by the computer user which can be changed at will. Microcomputers for commercial use usually contain at least 64k RAM (although new 16 bit micros contain up to 256k). Minicomputers contain at least 256k bytes and mainframes millions of bytes of RAM.

The speed with which a computer works is affected by the size of RAM available, as a long program will have to be split up into chunks if the whole program and data cannot all be contained in memory at the same time. Swapping parts of the program and data in and out takes time and thus slows down the time taken to process the program. Multi-user programs are made possibly by sharing memory between users. This further limits the amount of memory that can be allocated to each program. The computer is also slowed down by the need to service requests made by all the users. In reality the computer carries out part of each request and then moves on to the next user. This is called the Round Robin approach. To have a viable multi-user system a fast computer with a large memory is required, or the types of jobs that are done on the multi-user system can be limited to those not requiring a large amount of storage. Adding more terminals to a multi-user system will thus degrade the response of the computer. These points have to be borne in mind as they mean that it is not usually possible to improve a system simply by adding further terminals. Expansion can be achieved by networking whereby several similar computers are linked together to share peripheral equipment such as disc drives and printers. This allows the flexibility of shared facilities and communications between machines, but does require some of the computers' capacity to service the network.

If the power of the computer was limited to the amount of memory in the CPU then small computers would not be feasible. Extra memory where the CPU can quickly retrieve or store data is available in a variety of ways. These are largely differentiated by speed of access to the data and amount of data storage available. The worst is the home cassette recorder which is very slow and does not hold much data. It is not to be recommended for long term serious applicatons. Floppy discs can hold up to 1 megabyte (1 million bytes) of information, access is fairly quick and the reading heads can move immediately to the area holding the data (consider the speed with which you can locate a particular track of music on a record player, as against a tape recorder). Hard disc systems can contain a very large amount of data: 5 megabytes (one megabyte is a million bytes) would be a small system.

For archaeological use a hard disc is preferable, but in the event of financial difficulties could be put off to the second year. When buying a system, two disc drives will be more convenient to use than one, and will allow easy backup of data and programs which is an essential feature. It is also of benefit to buy at least one 8 inch floppy disc drive, as Single sided Single density 8 inch floppies are the only standard disc format. Having one will considerably ease problems of transferring data and programs between archaeological systems.

Terminals are a matter of choice, but green on black or yellow on brown screens are more gentle on the eyes. Seek the advice of an occupational health worker about the ergonomic factors in setting up the computer. This is important as there are important health consideration such as eye strain, stress and posture problems associated with the use of a computer terminal. In particular do not try to save money by using television screens as terminals for any extended period, as these are by far the worst for the eyes. A keyboard with a repeat key and function keys, which can be set by the user to run programs, is useful.

Printers come in a variety of forms. Performance is judged in speed of operation (characters printed per second, or CPS), quality of printing and durability. Dot matrix printers are fast and best for stock printout. The dots making up the characters are usually visible and thus not suitable for camera-ready copy or external mail (although more expensive dot matrix printers can be used for publications). The character sets are also usually not changeable. Most camera-ready copy is produced by daisy wheel printers, which are slow but produce high quality printing and have interchangeable fonts. These are well worth the extra cost and can improve the appearance of the organisation's publication and correspondence. Printers cost £200 to £2000. Try to buy one which takes wide printing paper, as many kinds of archaeological data can be expressed in columns. Wide paper allows more variables to be included conveniently, and it is paradoxically cheaper than A4 paper.

Graphic equipment is, on commercial systems, expensive but is worthy of investigation as archaeological data can often be presented either as a graph or image. Phase maps can be automatically produced at any scale by computer. Graphs and even pottery forms can be used to augment any report. You need a graphics board in your computer, a digitiser to turn pictures into numbers and a plotter to produce a paper copy of the image. This will cost about £2000 at current prices.

Micro-computers are adequate for providing a basic computer system for a Unit. A minimum system would consist of a micro-computer, terminal, double floppy disc system, and printer, and would cost around £2000.

Personal Computers

Personal computers are becoming cheaper and more and more powerful. They are limited by the size of their memories, the lack of computing languages available, speed of action, and availability of suitable software and of mass storage devices. However these are all improving and in the next few years will become more and more viable for serious use.

At present a micro-computer system will usually only have one terminal. Much of the time available on the computer will be spent on data collection (which is relatively undemanding on computer time). This limits, and competes for time with, analysis and programming. The personal computer system could provide a cheap but effective method of data capture. A system costing between £300 to £800 could provide the means to collect data and provide word processing facilities.

The feasibility of using personal computers will be tested in the next few months. Systems to look out for (Jan. 1984) are the Sinclair, the BBC and the Commodore 64. A micro-computer with an RS232 port will enable communications to be set up with the main computer data entry stations. Portable computers are improving all the time: the Epsom HX-20 is an attractive design with a built-in printer, small screen and cassette recorder.

The use of large mainframe computers is made possible to many archaeological organisations through their close contacts with local government or universities. They provide very powerful facilities for statistical and graphical work in particular. However in practice their use is problematic as it is difficult for the archaeological user to become familiar enough with the vast range of available programs and procedures to make full and effective use of the computer. The computer service is not tailored to the rather unusual type of work required by archaeologists and by and large using one's own computer is more profitable. However it is well worth establishing a communications link to the mainframe computer to take advantage of specialised programs. Thus standard processing would be carried out on the home computer which can then be packaged into the form required by mainframe computer programs and sent there for processing.

Software

To work a computer needs programs, and the most basic program is the operating system. This is the master control program which takes users' requests to run various programs, display data or programs on the screen, or print files. An operating system should be judged on three criteria: it should be easy to use, offer a comprehensive range of basic services, and there should be a lot of software available on the system. For micro-computers, CP/M is the industry standard and has a vast range of software available: a number of archaeological users are using it and building up a series of useful programs. If you are lucky enough to have a mini-computer get UNIX (or XENIX which is a form of UNIX): this operating system is a delight to work with. Unfortunately it makes working in CP/M seem very tedious by comparison! On a mainframe you will not have a choice.

The operating system will give you rudimentary programming facilites so that you can display, copy, print and maintain files. To go much further you will need to buy software packages or write programs yourself. There is no computing package which will enable one to do everything wanted without learning to program the computer. However packages can substantially reduce the amount of programming needing to be done. Buying software is difficult because it can only be fully appreciated after experience in using it. It may therefore be worth joining one of the software organisations which allows the hire of software first and subsequently its purchase if it is acceptable.

There is insufficient space to go into computer software in detail but one or two hints will be given. It is useful to purchase a data-base management system – these help to provide a retrieval sustem and keep data secure. Dbase2 is one such system which is available on CP/M. Whatever software you design or buy you should ensure that it will be able to do or help to do the following things:

Sorting

A sorting program should allow a file to be sorted by any combination of fields in the file. Thus a site index could be required, to be sorted for the county council by location first and then by period. The same file might be sorted for an archaeologist by period first and only secondly by location. This sorting should be possible using different field separators i.e. spaces, commas or semi-colons. Separators divide different data items, for example:

Context-1234, layer, grey, silt, roman, area a,

The sort should also allow whole files to be merged in the same sorting orders.

Searching

The computer system must allow information to be easily retrieved from the data files. A searching program will be required to do this. It is not necessary to start with a very sophisticated system as one which will find specified words in the data files is easy to provide. It can then be extended to look for more complicated expressions (for example using a thesaurus of technical terms).

Formatting

Files of data kept in the computer may not be in the ideal form to be printed and easily read. A formatting program which takes the information in the computer and prints it in an attractive form is very important. It is important that it is not restricted to any one format, so check how easy it is to change the format of output.

Updating

Some computer systems work very well but it is difficult to update the programs and/or data structure and any improvement is either put off or causes a disproportionate amount of effort. This is why computers get a bad name, as they can be used as an excuse to ossify working procedures. This is caused by bad computer programming and must be checked before purchase.

Editor

A text editor is very important. Sometimes the editor can be used in place of a program to make major transformations to data. Check that the editor allows automatic changes to be made to whole files and not just line by line. There should be a stream editing facility to allow programs to be edited by a predetermined set of instructions. For example data may be stored in a coded form but output may be wanted for an outside enquirer unfamiliar with one code. With a decent editor is is a simple matter (though care is needed to prevent unexpected results) to ask the computer to change all examples of GREE into GREEN or RPOT into ROMAN POTTERY for example. Word processing editors are also required to make the writing of reports as painless as possible (this report was prepared using WORD-STAR).

Joining

Try to ensure that files can be joined together to help analyse information coming from different original sources. Thus the finds work may first be done in isolation from the field work section. Later it will be necessary to analysis the finds from the perspective of the interpretation of the site. Thus one must either produce a monolithic and comprehensive data-base containing all archaeological information, or make a flexible system which will allow the easy conjunction of data for analysis. This means ensuring programs are flexible enough to work on data containing different information and in different formats. Without this flexibility the computer system can become horribly static.

Data Safety

As soon as data are entered into the computer it is imperative that a backup system should be set up. Any computer data storage medium is liable to corruption and it may not be possible to save the data which were on it. Therefore it is necessary to keep backup copies of all data and programs. Ideally you should keep three copies of all data, to ensure against disaster. Try to keep old copies of data as well. For example if you have 3 copies of a file which is said to contain all the Sites and Monuments information for the region, but someone accidently and without realising it erased most of the data you would have 3 identical copies of a virtually useless file. If 'Grandfather, Father and Son' backups are kept, when the 'Son' copy of the data is ruined it is possible to retrieve the 'Father' copy. This will be slightly out of date but most of the data will be saved.

Backup must be an automatic procedure and not one to put off, because without an efficient system a disaster could and probably will happen.

Collecting Data

Data collection is perhaps the most important aspect of the computer sytem. A common computer saying is "Rubbish In Rubbish Out", which is particularly appropriate for the archaeologist. Information in the computer must be consistent; staff using the system should be aware of the limitations of the data and the circumstances in which it was collected. There is a danger in computing of losing information without being aware of it. For example a request for all silt deposits in the Roman period will not receive information on silt deposits which have been misspelt or on Roman deposits which are incorrectly ascribed to another period. This is not more serious than the loss through misfiling of the paper copies of the data in the manual recording method, but as people tend to have undue respect for computers it may be more difficult to detect, and could have disastrous effects upon analysis. It is therefore necessary to set up rigorous checking procedures, which should be based both on returning the information recording by computer to the person doing the recording (or preferably someone else in a position to check the data), to check the veracity of the information recorded. When writing computer programs it is important to check the consistency of data – checking that keywords in certain fields are valid and that data which cross-refers to elsewhere is correctly cross referenced. This is vital and cannot be skimped.

This process can be helped by a well thought out data collection strategy. The first decision in preparing the computer system is the form in which the data will be stored in the computer. The following are possible ways of organising data entry:

Tagged Data

> *con 2314 *typ fill
> *tone dark *coladj greeny *col grey
> *partadj silty *part clay

This method is used by the Museum Documentation Association for their computer system. It has the disadvantage that the person entering data has more typing to do, but it allows data to be entered in any order and copes easily with missing data. Retrieval of selected information is made easier by the presence of tags. Thus one can very easily ask to printout all, for example, particle sizes.

Formatted Data

> 2314 fill dark greeny grey silty clay
> 2315 fill mid brown silt

This method is helpful in that data are easy to compare as the position in the file determines the meaning of the entry. It is easy to scan the file for errors or to find data. However it is usually tedious to collect because of the need to type spaces (or tabs) to line data up correctly. It is more normally used for formatting output than for collecting data.

Punctuated Data

    2314/fill/dark greeny-grey silty-clay/
    2315/fill/mid brown silt/

This form is very flexible and compact. Missing information is simply recorded by absence of data between punctuation marks. Staff must however know the order and form in which data are collected. It is therefore recommended that this form is only used by those very familiar with the data and for storing information compactly in the computer. Once information is in the computer in this form it is easy to write and use sorting and formatting programs to handle the data. It is possible to handle more complicated subdivisions of the data using this method. One can either allow one field (area between punctuation – or field separators – in this case '/') per item or combine this with more advanced string handling techniques. For example in the case above the third field which is the soil description can if required be further split up using spaces as secondary field separators. The first item is the tone, the second item is the colour and the third is the particle type. The second and third items can be further separated by the hyphens into 'adjectives' (greeny, silty) and main items (grey, silt).

Question and Answer

    Context no? 2314
    Type of deposit? fill
    Tone of colour? dark
    Colour? greeny-grey
    Particle Size? silty-clay

The question and answer approach is very useful as it can be used to guide staff through the data entry system. It is possible to program the computer so that only certain keywords or number ranges are accepted by the computer. It can therefore be a great help in ensuring the coherency of data recorded by different people.

Free Text

    2314 fill dark greeny grey silty clay
    2315 fill mid brown silt

Free text can be used to collect data but it can be dangerous as no control is imposed on the data collected. It also needs fairly complicated computer

41

programs either to interpret data as it is entered, or to set up a comprehensive retrieval system which will not omit important information, or conversely return too much information (false drops) when the data are interrogated.

Coded Text

```
2314 1 23 34 46 51 62
2315 1 22 45 61
```

Coded text uses numbers or characters to represent data. The example above corresponds to the free text entry. The advantages are reduction of the amount of typing necessary and the amount of computer storage required. The disadvantage is the difficulty of reading the data. This makes data entry more liable to error and may slow it down. Decoding programs need to be writen.

A compromise is to code in more readable form.

```
2314 fill dark gree grey silt clay
2315 fill mid brow silt
```

A four figure code is usually enough to make the code easy to remember and read. However the data compression is not very great.

These methods are by no means mutually exclusive as viable combinations can work very well. For example a question and answer program may use a four letter code with free text answers for comments.

If there is a large staff who may not be completely familiar with the data collected, or the order in which it was collected, then a question and answer program is the best to use. It has the advantage that such a program will check the data as it is entered into the computer and will prompt the user if they are not sure which data to enter. It has the disadvantage of being relatively slow once staff have become very familiar with the data. Jonathan Moffet at the Institute of Archaeology has written a data entry stem with Dr Graham which allows an inexperienced computer user to write their own question and answer programs very quickly. At the museum we use ths question and answer package to collect data gathered by large numbers of our staff. If members of staff have their own project or are in charge of a particular branch of data collection then they collect data in the punctuated form. This form is ideally suited for writing simple programs to manipulate data. Fixed field input is only to be recommended if a special form entry program is available.

Data Collection Devices

A great deal of time can be saved by the use of data collection devices. For example one can buy data pads which allow paper forms to be used to input data. Areas on the pad are programmed so that they represent certain information. Thus fairly complicated data can be entered using a single touch of the pad. Recording the following bulk finds information would be achieved by 9 touches:

Context 2345 5 cardboard boxes Roman Pottery and Building Materials.

(four of these are for the context number). This method also has the advantage that spelling mistakes are automatically avoided and that a paper copy is provided in case of machine or human failure. Similar devices can be attached to the screen of the computer and touch sensitive areas allow the user to run through a program without needing to know how to type. These have the advantage over the pad that they can be more directly run by a program which is not limited by the amount of information held on paper. Both of these devices can be used in tandem with a keyboard so that numbers and free text can be entered easily. Computer packages are available which allow data entry using forms displayed on the screen and are well worth the cost if no data entry devices are available.

A decision must be made on who is to enter data into the computer. Employing specialist data entry staff provides fast typists who soon get to know the structure and composition of the data they are collecting. However they have the disadvantage of distancing data collection staff from the computer. Using the normal finds and excavation staff to enter data has the advantage of familiarising staff with data recording methods and encouraging staff to use the computer. This has a feedback effect whereby staff are self educated in the correct method of recording information for the computer. It eases the task of transferring data from the written record to the computer record as they should be recorded similarly by the same people. The museum has adopted this latter approach and considerable improvement in basic recording has been achieved.

Staff

Having a specialist computer programmer who is also familiar with archaeological recording is a great advantage. The purchase of computing equipment should be accompanied by a staff training scheme in the use of computers. Time and money should be provided for the attendance of evening classes and courses. This is necessary to make the fullest use of the computer.

Future Developments

Computers will become a standard feature of life in the next 10 years. Virtually all data will be stored in computers and staff can write all reports and correspondence using word processing facilities on computers. Data exchange will become far easier as telephone and cable links enable remote computers to be linked. This will finally end the appalling difficulties facing exchange of data between computer systems. Personal computer systems will soon be viable for serious applications. The vast market provided by the proliferation of computers will provide outlets for software and hardware volume sales. This will substantially reduce the cost and provide much enhanced computer facilities. It will also provide the stimulus for the production of cheaper and better data entry facilities. We can expect in the next few years to get portable data entry devices to enable data capture in the field at a price sufficiently low to plan for the abolition of the paper copy form as an intermediate stage in data collection. This will substantially reduce the cost of computing and we can expect excavation staff to record both context sheets and plans by computer quickly at a low cost. The true benefits of computerisation will only be realised when the coverage of data held in computers is comprehensive and can easily be exchanged between computers. Thus in the early years the return from computerisation will be reduced. Money will need to be spent in entering the backlog of archaeological data into computers. Thus previous sites, reports, bibliographies, and Sites and Monuments records will need to be recorded on computer to exploit fully the potential of computer filing systems.

Central government holds the key to this advance as archaeology needs a clear commitment to the setting up of comprehensive computer systems for archaeological organisations. The Dept of the Environment for instance could provide funds for a fundamentaly important data exchange centre which would enable data and programs to be exchanged easily between archaeological users. This would be cost effective as it would make more efficient use of information recorded, reduce duplication of data collection, facilitate exchange of information in the archaeological world and reduce the time spent duplicating archaeological computer programs.

The DOE must also fund data collection by computer for the backlog of archaeological information. Without a direct initiative the utility of archaeological computer systems will be less than the revolutionary change it should be.

Conclusion

Organisations using the computer will greatly improve their production of reports and publications. The computer will allow more attention to be paid to research and synthetic projects without exorbitant costs. Computers will improve efficiency but will probably not reduce employment levels as necessary work will take up any time freed by the use of computer. More fundamental changes await improvement in communication between computer systems.

CHAPTER 4

DATA CATCHMENT ANALYSIS AND COMPUTER CARRYING CAPACITY

NOTES ON THEORY AND PRACTICE OF THE USE OF COMPUTER SYSTEMS IN ARCHAEOLOGY

A. Voorrips

Albert Egges van Giffen Instituut

voor Prae- en Protohistorie

Universiteit van Amsterdam

'Then I took one mighty step, and I fell right on my ass'

(Dory Previn)

Archaeologists and big computer systems

Since the late sixties, a revolution in quantitative techniques has taken place in archaeology. This revolution has had many implications for archaeological theory and method, but could not and would not have happened without the simultaneous development of computer hardware, computer languages and computer programs. Data input mediums have progressed from paper tape to punched cards, to tape cartridges, to disks. Data output mediums have gone from slow typewriters to noisy printers, to coolly shining display screens; control languages have developed from machine code to assemblers, to high level programming languages, to user-oriented command languages. In the seventies, computer hardware development entered a new phase – the chip became the cheap but sophisticated heart of computer systems. An enormous and profitable market opened up for everybody who liked to tinker in his basement, and a great variety of micro-computers entered the scene, their quality ranging from absolutely crummy to moderately solid and reliable. Over the last twelve years I have been in a position which enabled me to follow the developments in computer systems and to evaluate their usefulness in archaeological enterprises by putting them to work in the contexts of archaeological analysis, field work, and data management.

The recent emphasis on the use of micro-computers in archaeology is an interesting new development, but it is also a development which makes me worry. I am worried – *not* about archaeology, *not* about micro-computers, but about the combination of archaeologist and micro-computer. To me it seems that this combination might make all of the mistakes and get into all of the dead ends which a previous generation of scientists – including archaeologists – did when they began to cope with computer systems called 'big' about twenty years ago. What really happened when, for the first time, archaeologists discovered computers? The machine, put forward as the cure for most, if not all of the archaeologists' problems, proved to be a beast which was difficult to tame. First of all, one had to learn at least one more or less complicated programming language, and at least one complicated operating system. Second, as soon as the large amounts of data, considered normal by archaeologists, had to be manipulated, most systems produced the equivalents of little blue flames and smoke clouds, indicating that it was really too much for them. Third, when an archaeologist formulated his analytical question, more often than not it became clear that for his problem there either did not exist an appropriate approach, or that with the system *he* was using there were no programs available that would suit his needs. Fourth, even when programs *did* exist, it happened quite often that some time later a message reached the archaeologist that on further inspection and checking the program did not behave exactly like it should – which was a nice way of saying that it produced garbage. In fact, in most cases the archaeologist would have found that out already – either by getting messages from the system operator like: 'don't do this ever again' (after a program causing a system crash), or because he got output which was voluminous and utterly incomprehensible. Finally, at regular or irregular intervals, but too often anyway, a message would reach the archaeologist that because of a 'hardware fault' his data – the product of many days of card punching and error correction – had been lost and could not be recovered. It is not amazing that the reaction of many archaeologists was never to get close to a computer again.

That was fifteen years ago. Today, the beast has been tamed rather well, and things are quite a bit better. Big computer systems are *really* big now, and they will swallow great amounts of data without trouble, even the enormous amounts archaeologists tend to produce. Operating systems have grown much more 'user friendly', and the need for knowing programming languages has strongly diminished. There are many program packages readily available now for all kinds of purposes. Most of these packages use simple command languages, and they provide for most, if not all the needs of the average archaeologist. By now these packages have been thoroughly

46

tested, and lead rarely to disastrous results – which is different from meaningless results, the latter being caused by meaningless data or meaningless manipulations. Loss of data which reside on a big computer system is practically extinct because of the elaborate back-up procedures which are part of the normal, day by day actions performed by such a system. In fact, the archaeologist's data may be lost and recovered without him even noticing it.

The attitude of the computer people themselves, from system manager to operator, has changed as well. One of the great advantages of big computer systems has always been that the user does not have to worry about starting up the system or about its maintenance and performance. However, in the beginning of the computer era, user complaints about the system were considered a scarcely tolerated form of blasphemy by the computer people. By now, it is understood and accepted that the user is a customer, without whom the existence of the whole computer system loses its credibility. To an extent this is not only true for the user in his relation to the system people, but also for the system people in their relation to the computer manufacturer. Present day mainframes are not exactly an article which is sold over the counter. Neither were the big systems of fifteen years ago, but competition has become harder. You do not have to sell that many five million pound systems to keep you going as a manufacturer, but it is worthwhile keeping your customers happy – they *might* switch to another brand after the period during which you, contractually, have to provide maintenance and debugging. Taking all of this together, the conclusion should be that, for an archaeologist today, the use of a big, well established computer system is an easy, reliable, resourceful, and not too expensive way of data storage, data analysis, and information retrieval.

Archaeologists and micro-computers – how not to do it

The micro-computers of today are comparable with the big systems of fifteen years ago. They have about the same capacity – something from 32K to 128K bytes. They present the user with the same kinds of problems as well, even with a few more. An archaeologist who buys a micro-computer has to take care of all kinds of tasks which have nothing to do with the data analysis or information retrieval he wants to use his system for, but which are necessary to get and to keep the system running. This means learning a number of new trades – those of system analyst, system manager, programmer, and operator – from manuals which are characterised by their obscurity and incompleteness. The learning process may be completed by taking some expensive courses organised by the system seller. The main outcome is more often than not an overall sense of bafflement. The software which is obtained from the manufacturer is frequently not very good. It is clearly not written with the needs of archaeologists in mind. After all, the market for micro-computers is in business and entertainment, and not in science. Most micro-computers speak some local dialect of BASIC – a language which is unsuitable for anything but the most primitive applica-

47

tions. Compatibility between the various BASIC dialects is moderate at best, which means that conversion of programs is a time and effort consuming operation. The quality of compilers for FORTRAN or PASCAL leaves much to be desired, given that such compilers even exist. On many occasions they seem to be in an eternal state of being announced by the manufacturer. For most archaeological applications, the storage capacity of a micro-computer is too small, and expensive additional storage has to be purchased as well. Statistical packages and data management programs for micro-computers are slow, primitive, and not well tested. In case of problems, both with the hardware and with the software, the maintenance by the manufacturer or his representatives tends to be of low quality – because of lack of knowledge, lack of interest, or both. This is not surprising, of course. A micro-computer *is* a mass product, and it is also a status object. The policy of trying to sell a new model instead of repairing the older one – well known to us in the case of cars, television sets, refrigerators, and electric washers – has been firmly established in the micro-computer branch as well. Archaeologists have to write their own programs, if not operating systems, for about everything they want to do on a micro-computer. Apart from the fact that such programs often will be badly structured, slow, and not fool proof, one might wonder whether an archaeologist should not better spend his time doing archaeology. Now, instead of trying to be a good archaeologist, the person with the micro-computer is his own bad systems analyst, his own bad programmer, and his own bad operator. In the end he probably produces bad archaeology as well. . . .

An additional danger is the gain in prestige and power a micro-computer seems to provide for its boss. The magic of computers still has not worn out among archaeologists. Like fifteen years ago, when one had to kneel down before the priests of the big computer system, *now* the colleagues of a 'micro-boss' have to kneel down before him to get the data processed they entrusted to him in a moment of temporary insanity. However attractive this role of micro-boss may be to some archaeologists, the situation can not be called a development; it should be classified as a regression to computer-infancy.

The conclusion must be that the policy of replacing the use of a big computer system by the use of a local, independent micro-computer should be avoided as much as possible. If, after a thorough check, it proves to be impossible to gain access to a big computer system and the decision is made to purchase a micro-computer, the archaeologists involved have to realize that at least one of them must stop doing archaeology and must devote himself totally to the micro-computer. This will mean a complete re-education in applied information science, years of trouble, and no guarantee for smooth data processing in the future.

Archaeologists and micro-computers – how to do it

Micro-computers can not and should not be considered machines which can

48

replace the big computer systems, but they must be seen as welcome and valuable *additions* to those mainframes. Additions in the form of *data entry units* and *single purpose machines,* can be linked to big systems and then function as intelligent *communication devices.* Such usage prevents the building or buying of extensive low quality software in the field of data analysis; it prevents the purchasing of expensive additional storage in the field of data-bases and data management as well as the wild growth of incompatible data handling systems. Word processing is rapidly becoming a major function of micro-computers. Thanks to the fact that word processing capacity is a strong requirement in the world of business micro-computers, most brands do provide reasonable to sophisticated word processing packages. When we take into account the time and costs involved in the preparing of archaeological reports with the help of secretaries (if available!) and typewriters, the use of a micro-computer with a good word processing package often will mean a substantial decrease of publication costs and a substantial increase in publication speed. An example of the use of a micro-computer as a single purpose machine is in the field of interactive computer graphics. Most big systems consider this application too expensive and too big a strain on the system to make it a normal part of their services. Here then we might speak of a specific archaeological need which can not be solved adequately by the use of a big system and for which an independent micro-computer might be a solution. The main function, however, of micro-computers in archaeology is their use as data entry units. The intelligence of the micro-computer is used to monitor the 'off line' data entry, both alphanumeric and graphic; some preliminary sorting and printing can be performed, and then, linking the micro-computer to a big host system, the 'clean' data can be transmitted quickly for further storage in a data-base. From the data-base information can be retrieved, be it for administrative purposes (like catalogues) or for analytical ones.

The design of a well-functioning data entry system is not a task to be taken lightly, however. The quality and practicality of a data entry system for archaeological field work is first of all dependent on the overall research design and logistics under which the field work is carried out, and only secondarily on the technicalities of the micro computer. In the next section of this paper, some of the more general problems which must be solved will be discussed.

Computerised data entry in archaeological field work

Three different 'information flows' can generally be distinguished in an archaeological project. There is, first of all, the data set which contains the information on 'where does it come from', like coordinates, feature designations, and so on. The administrative labelling of *it,* a labelling which will be repeated – by man or machine – in all other data sets, must also be included in the first data set. The second flow contains the information on 'what is it (for), and how many are there of it', for example '23 sherds, five bones and two pieces of wood' – the result of digging out a feature –, or 'one bronze pin', or 'one soil sample for the study of particle size'. The third flow contains the information specific to a particular find category and/or to a particular research method. Pottery is analysed in a different way from pollen samples, or charcoal, and so on. The various information flows do not occur simultaneously. Flow number one, the 'field information', is the first. Flow number two, the 'field lab information', comes in sometime later after the cleaning, numbering, counting, weighing and broad categorisation of the finds. Flow number three, the 'specialist's data', may come in after some more days, or weeks, or years. . . .

In the field it is crucial to have flows one and two under control – to have them entered, checked, perhaps reformatted, perhaps sorted and printed – and to have them transmitted to the host computer system and entered into the existing data-base structure. Regardless of whether the data-base structure has been defined specifically for the field work in question or is pre-existing, it must be possible to check in the field whether or not the entry into the data-base of the field information has been successful.

The processing of flows one and two by means of a field computer has some specific problems. The first one is the *lack of redundancy* in the data entry phase, as compared to the 'classic' methods of manually recording information in books or on lists. In the manual approach, lots of errors and omissions get corrected almost automatically by the people who fill out and copy lists – they glance over the pages, they notice the implausibilities and impossibilities, and they correct them right away. Copying is in itself a source of error as well, but the net effect of manual data entry is that the data have passed a large number of checks before they are 'official'. Quite another picuture emerges when data entry is performed by means of the computer keyboard. There are no visible lists to which the data are added, and no manual copies will be made. The redundancy, produced by the multiple times that eyes of archaeologists look at the data in the manual approach, has gone.

A computerised data entry system therefore must perform the necessary checks by itself, as far as possible. The data entry must be *monitored,* and immediate plausibility checks must be exercised by the monitoring program. The technicalities of such a monitoring program will partially depend on the specific data entry device – it makes a world of difference if one uses a video display or a typewriter-like device. There are two main types of control, however. The first one is on the *syntax* of the data records entered – checks on number of entries per record, numerical or alphabetical characters, and so on. The second one is the check on the *content* – when the dig takes place at about 10 m above sea level, a level of minus 5 m in a record might be wrong. The check on content can be performed by using an interactive data entry program that requests the limiting values of the various measurements at the beginning of each data entry session, and that checks each entry against those values before accepting it. Assuming that larger blocks of records will be kept in local memory before being transmitted to an external storage device, further overall checks, in particular those for double used find numbers, must be performed by the program before each transmission and at each update of the (host computer-located) data-base. While these procedures do not guarantee error-free data, the number of errors becomes comparable with the number of errors made under manual data entry, and in general it will be less. It is sometimes advocated that only the archaeologist responsible for a batch of data should enter it. His knowledge of the data and their context would diminish the chances of impossible or implausible entries being made, and the use of a monitoring program would be superfluous. The procedure would further guarantee that the archaeologist understands what is happening to his data when they get into a computer.

This approach has its benefits indeed, but, in particular in large excavations, it may be impractical from a logistical point of view. Moreover, even intimate knowledge of the data does not provide a guarantee against typing errors. . . ! In situations where the data entry is not performed by the excavator himself, it is important that the various 'data producers' have a fair idea about what is going to happen to their data, and about the possibilities and restrictions of the data entry system. An appropriate chapter in the excavation handbook and a demonstration of the data entry system must always be provided by the organisers of the project.

The second general problem in computerised data entry and data storage is the *prevention of loss of data*. This problem is encountered at three levels. The lowest level is that of the data entry itself. No typing error of whatever strange kind should lead to a program abort and consequent loss of data which is already typed in and not yet stored away. Furthermore, commands from the man at the keyboard to finish a data entry session should always trigger a check as to whether entered data have indeed been stored safely, and if not, appropriate messages must be displayed or printed. However trivial these conditions may sound, to get a data entry program 'fool proof' is in most cases much harder than to build in various checks on syntax and content.

The second level on which attention must be paid to the prevention of loss of data is that of the *local back up*. It is an absolute requirement that after each data entry session at least one local copy is made of the data entered. After all, hardware errors *do* sometimes occur, in particular on storage devices which are used in non-office circumstances. The third level on which to take action to prevent loss of data is that of the *remote back up*. We may assume that data transmission itself will be checked automatically by the sending and/or receiving system. Checks on the appropriate storing of data in the remote data-base should also be performed. Moreover, despite the fact that big systems do have good recovery procedures, it is worth making and keeping at least one extra copy of the data-base, for instance on magnetic tape, and to store a master copy in a different place. Computer centres *can* burn down. . . . Again, these things sound rather trivial, but given a choice for computerised data entry and data storage, the copies on paper of the archaeological data no longer exist in the number and the detail of manual systems, and archaeologists should be strongly aware of that.

Archaeological data management systems

The term 'data-base' has come up a number of times already in this paper, and in this section I will specify somewhat the types of data-bases which are of use to archaeologists. It is better to talk of data *management systems* than of data-bases. A data-base is a body of data which has been organized and which is accessible by means of a data management system. The system provides the *structure* of the data-base. The choice of data management system depends on the use to be made of the data-base.

In excavation situations, the data-base will have to function as the structured data pool from which data for *analysis* can be readily extracted. It is not the single item or object which is of interest – as in many museum-type applications – but *the shared or non-shared characteristics* of various kind of items, the *dispersion of items* over the three dimensional space plotted during the excavation, and the *spatial correlations* among different kinds of items, or between certain features and items. It is therefore more important that an excavation data management system can produce files which are ready to serve as input for statistical and spatial analysis program packages, and it is less important that beautiful catalogues can be generated. The reverse will be true in the case of the use of computerised data management for administering the cultural heritage, where the emphasis lies on the ability to produce quickly the whereabouts and the assumed archaeological importance of any single archaeological object, or series or objects.

The choice of data management system must be made with this difference of purpose in mind, in particular because the two types of requirements lead to different data-base structures. A data management system is either 'case-oriented', or 'variable-oriented', the former being the museum choice, the latter being the analyst's choice. Case-oriented data management systems generally provide us with better capacities for the handling of textual information, while variable-oriented data management systems more easily produce output which can serve as input for analytical program packages or can even perform a number of analyses themselves. In both cases however, good data management systems tend to use lots of storage and central memory space. There is an inverse relationship between the amount of space used and the speed at which information can be retrieved. One thing is clear however. Given the enormous importance of data management systems in nearly every field of science, business and adminis-tration, and given the refined data management systems which already exist, it is unnecessary for archaeologists to develop their own systems. It would be a waste of time. The best policy for the archaeologist is to find a data-base managment system among the many existing ones which will allow him to create the data-base structure he needs. Energy is better spent getting such a data management system implemented on a host computer than constructing some weird, restricted data management system of one's own.

I would like to make a final comment on the use of data management systems in archaeology. Two streams are visible in Britain, continental Europe, and the U.S.A. The first stream is more or less strongly sponsored by the governments and is concerned almost exclusively with the creation of data-bases of the 'cultural heritage', which are object-oriented. The second stream gets much less official sponsoring. It consists of archaeologists who want to use the modern technological aids to assist them in their task of *understanding* cultural heritage – not as a loose collection of queer events, but as the material outcomes of behavioural processes. The two streams have not yet met, but hopefully they will sometime. They only *can* come together when all people concerned can share and can use the data, collected and described by any one of them. And the latter will only become possible by a judicious and sensible use of advanced information technology.

Conclusions

It is fascinating to practise archaeology in these days of rapidly expanding possibilites in data storage, data retrieval and data analysis. However, to be an archaeologist now puts the responsibility on our shoulders to incorporate as well as we can the exciting new tools into the daily practice of archaeology. This means that we must estimate coolly and critically which of the many technical gadgets will, in the long run, serve archaeology best.

In my opinion, the most promising new development is the expansion of easily accessible computer networks. Such networks provide us with a choice of mainframes, of methods for analysis, and of data management systems. The dependency on a single mainframe, often a reason for the purchase of a micro-computer, can be abolished. Finally, the freedom of choice which we users get by subscribing to one or more networks, also leads towards an intensified competition between the various mainframes for the consumer's favour. And that is just the way in which we, computer-using archaeologists like it!

CHAPTER 5

INFORMATION TECHNOLOGY: APPLICATION BY THE DYFED ARCHAEOLOGICAL TRUST

Don Benson

Dyfed Archaeological Trust

The Dyfed Archaeological Trust is one of four organisations identically constituted and established in 1975-6 by the DOE Ancient Monuments Branch (Wales), now the Conservation and Land Division of the Welsh Office, as part of the coherent arrangements for rescue Archaeology in Wales. My own experience of information technology is entirely non-technical, though I am grateful for the (largely unsuccessful) attempts of colleagues Joe Jefferies (DOE Central Excavation Unit) and Charles Stenger (the Trust's Record Officer) to educate me in these areas. Instead, I must rely on a long-standing interest and belief in the assistance that computers can give in the routine handling and processing of archaeological information, and on the Trust's experience with its own equipment over the last two years. This experience should be seen in the context of a comparatively small archaeological unit (seven full-time staff) working in a predominantly rural area on a relatively low budget – circumstances which dictate a more modest approach to the application of information technology than we would wish, or a larger organisation might be able to afford.

As far as information collection and management are concerned, there are probably more differences between the Welsh Trusts than similarities, although some of these differences reflect different circumstances in each area – for example, the state of R.C.H.A.M. inventory work, the presence of a County Archaeologist, and so on. Each Trust's *excavation* recording system is different in detail, though three of the Trusts employ similar recording forms. For Sites and Monuments Records work, three Trusts (Gwynedd is the exception) use almost identical Site Record Forms, providing in the long term a good foundation for easier information exchange. At present, Dyfed is the only Trust with its own computer equipment. The Clwyd-Powys Trust has arrangements with the Archaeology Officer in the Clwyd County Planning Department for processing data on a mainframe computer. No such arrangements exists in Powys, and the Trust is currently examining its requirements for computer facilities for that area. The Glamorgan-Gwent Trust has no computer facilities, although computer processing of S.M.R. data is an objective. None of the Trusts at present have 'in house' experience of computer processing of *excavation* records, although Dyfed is just beginning to acquire this. The Gwynedd Trust has used University facilities from time to time to assist in special analysis of some material from excavations.

Outside the Trusts there are several other bodies involved in the collection of archaeological information. These include the National Museum of Wales, a small number of Local Authority Museums, and the Welsh Office – for scheduled Ancient Monuments and Listed Buildings work; monument inventory work and the maintenance of the National Monuments Record (Wales) is of course the function of the R.C.A.H.M. None of these bodies, however, are applying computers to the collection, management and dissemination of archaeological information, although several museums are using M.D.A. record cards. Nor has any overall national (i.e. Welsh) structure or strategy for the application of computers to archaeological problems been discussed, although as a result of the 'Heseltine proposals', it may be that attention will be focussed on these areas in the near future.

The background to the Dyfed Trust's involvement in computer work has been outlined elsewhere (Stewart 1980). It owes much to the interest of both myself and Joe Jefferies of the DOE Central Excavation Unit in computer applications to archaeological records several years ago, prior to the establishment of the Trust; and more recently to continuing co-operation between the Trust and the Central Excavation Unit. From the time of the Trust's establishment in 1975 it has been deliberate policy to apply computer power to assist in Trust activities. Record forms designed for computer input of both excavation and S.M.R. data have been employed from the beginning, but it has taken a long time to translate theory into working practice. Contributory factors include a translation from an experimental system using the Honeywell mainframe computer time sharing service, to a system based on a micro-computer; the development of versatile software (especially the creation of a data-base structure independent of any machine system); the lack of funds for equipment purchase, and the uncertainty about developments in the micro-computer field itself.

We were eventually able to acquire a micro-computer (an R.M.L. 380Z with two 8 inch floppy discs) in 1979. For the first nine months the equipment was lent to the Central Excavation Unit for software development. An untrained member of the Trust's staff spent ten weeks with the C.E.U. acquiring experience of operation and programming work and assisting in software development. Over the last 21 months we have been processing the backlog of Sites and Monuments Record data. This has involved editing the original data, generating secondary files, producing catalogues and refining catalogue organisation. We also added a further

1500 sites to our records, bringing the total up to 10,000. Editing the original data has taken an unnecessarily large proportion of time, since the data-base, originally commercially prepared for us on punch cards for use on a Honeywell mainframe system, was found to contain many input errors. Had we had our own micro-computer at that stage, entering the same amount of data directly would have been much quicker.

Until recently Sites and Monuments Record work has monopolised the use of equipment, and only now are we turning our attention to applying it for other purposes. In fact the range of *desirable* applications covers almost all aspects of the Trust's work – in the collection, processing and dissemination of information from excavation and survey; in planning long-term excavation and survey strategies, in assessing the importance of individual sites; in the preparation and operation of planning control systems and in the input of information into Structure and Local Plans; in the stimulation of voluntary activity; in the preparation of report texts (using word processing facilities) and in internal administration and accounting.

But this is far too long a shopping list, and even in the limited areas in which we use our micro-computers we have found that competition has very quickly developed between data input requirements (i.e. collection/ data capture), sorting, processing, editing, routine catalogue production and software development work. This is not a problem primarily related to the processing or storage capacities of any individual machine, but simply of access to the keyboard – or not enough keyboards. The sort of equipment one requires will be dictated mainly by the volume of data to be collected and how quickly it can, and needs to be processed. A single micro-computer will generally only be of use for one project, or even part of one project; one also where the 'turn-around' time in handling data is not an important consideration. Even on a single excavation, competition for keyboard access between data input and processing may well become a problem, especially if results need to be fed back to site staff regularly and quickly. And if more than one excavation requires this kind of service at the same time, and there are regular demands from other sources as well, then plainly one micro-computer is not enough.

A distinction needs to be drawn between data collection and data processing requirements; separate equipment should be employed for these purposes. It is important to consider not which is the best single micro-computer to acquire, but what is the best configuration of equipment to suit the circumstances. Capital and maintenance costs will be major factors in the choice of equipment, but not the only ones. Even if we could afford it, we would not favour using our disc-based equipment on site; although such equipment is portable, its environmental tolerance is limited. Our experience is that this kind of equipment is best kept in one place, if breakdowns are to be minimized.

Bearing in mind our purse, and that the majority of our excavations are carried out in rural areas and conditions, we have for some time been searching for low-cost equipment which could be used independently for

56

collecting data which would then be transferred and processed on our office based machine. Fortunately Research Machines Limited have now developed a smaller micro-computer – a 480Z LINK – which can be used independently or linked directly to the larger 380Z equipment, forming part of a 'network' system. We have recently purchased two 480Z's (basic cost, a little over £500 each) and also substituted for the standard cassette storage system (which is slow to access data and tedious to transfer to disc), a high speed digital cassette system (IKON F.V.1) designed to transfer data from one computer to another. This equipment has its own microprocessor based operating system functioning at about ten times the speed of a conventional cassette system. Whilst this whole arrangement will be slower than the use of a configuration based entirely on disc equipment, less than a third of the capital outlay for the latter is involved. Inevitably, our approach is a compromise with regard to available finance, but in an 'either/or' situation, we prefer to enhance our data collection capacity rather than our existing processing capacity. By this means we hope to relieve the present blockage at the collection end, provide greater flexibility of data management, and, because of R.M.L.'s development policy, have capacity for expansion in the future.

As far as the use of micro-computers for dissemination of information is concerned, our experience relates only to the use of hard copy catalogues, although we are discussing the transfer of data to our nearest University computer, with links to the regional Universities Computer Network, which in turn in the not too distant future may figure in a country wide sytem, offering enormous potential for information distribution and exchange. The technology for disseminating information in a variety of ways and on a grand scale certainly exists, and is improving all the time, but at present, financial and organisational problems within archaeology itself provide a barrier to the application and development of this technology on a national and regional level. Formulation of clear objectives and central direction are both needed to complement the present localised and predominantly local initiatives. Otherwise, locally, there seems little point in utilising information technology beyond certain limits – no virtue in taking a technological sledge hammer to crack an archaeological nut just the sake of it. In these circumstances, catalogue production and distribution seem likley to make the most useful contribution to the dissemination of archaeological information in the immediate future.

Certainly the facility to reproduce information quickly in hard copy form, especially for Sites and Monuments infomation, has made a tremendous difference to the Trust's work. For example, a selection of site data ordered by 1:10,000 sheets, usually in the form of sigle line entry catalogues, is supplied to Local Planning Authorities for development control purposes, and the same data are supplied in a period and site type order to back up written statements submitted for Local Plans. In other cases, catalogues containing full data are supplied where the Planning Authority wishes and is able to use it in a responsible manner. Parish and/or

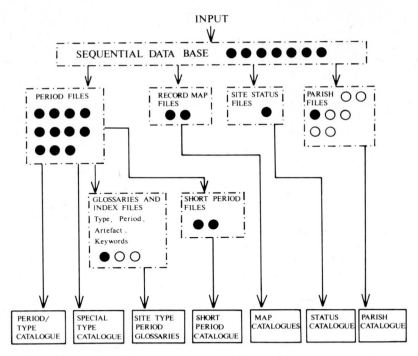

Fig. 1 Relationships between computer files and printed catalogues at the Dyfed Archaeological Trust.

quarter sheet catalogues are made available to local field-workers as a basis for fieldwork in the hope that this will result in some feedback to the Trust. Requests for information on a period, area, or site type basis, from researchers within or outside the County are answered by the supply of a relevant catalogue. These may be rather obvious examples, but they have all been made possible through having our own micro-computer. Time, rather than facilities permitting, we would like to circulate glossaries as short indexes to the information the Trust holds, and generate bibliographical data taken directly from the source record on our site index. A long-standing objective is to publish a summary of the archaeology of the county backed up by period catalogues, perhaps in microfiche form. This would go some way towards satisfying our obligations towards both the general public and also the academic sectors.

As far as our internal retrieval requirements are concerned, again most of these are satisfied in the first instance by reference to a standard series of standard catalogues – e.g. Period (sub-order Site Type); Parish; Artefacts; Record Map Index (1:10,000 scale sheets). Copies of the latter are physically attached to each Record Map and edited versions are attached to archaeological constraint maps. 'Short form' catalogues are also produced, e.g. for Scheduled Monuments, enabling for instance quick correlation of Welsh Office reference numbers with our own site numbers. The Period Catalogues are the only ones in which we include all the data on our index, and to individual site records in these catalogues will also be added, by merging and creating new computer files, summary information on contexts, artefacts and site records from excavated sites. The Period Catalogues will also then provide a cross-index to more detailed catalogues produced as part of the processing of excavation records and the creation of an excavation archive.

From time to time other catalogues are produced at the request of Trust staff working on particular subjects. We find that these catalogues generally generate good 'feedback' since the recipient is in a better position to correct errors and update the basic data, than someone less familiar with that particular area of research. For most other enquiries, an enquirer will often start with one of the standard indexes or catalogues and proceed to another as more detailed information is required, until it becomes necessary to consult original records. We find no retrieval difficulties with this approach. It is not necessary to interrogate the relevant computer disc directly when it takes only a couple of minutes to look something up in a catalogue. There are times, as mentioned above, when the combination of data required would be tedious to extract manually from standard catalogues. But I find it hard to think of an instance in such cases where the enquirer has not wanted a good deal of data in hard copy output which he can then take away and study at his convenience. Whilst a larger computer with a sophisticated data-base system might produce in minutes information that may require an hour's work on our equipment, this hardly matters when, without any sort of computer, the information required might take days or even weeks to obtain.

Efficient processing and effective retrieval is a matter of scale. In our case, both these aspects would be improved by a hard disc system, since with only the 500K on-line storage capacity on floppy disc, data has to be spread over several discs. But in practice this is not so much of a handicap as it may seem. Our Sites and Monuments Record data (which excludes descriptive text) in sequential order represents some 2.5 megabytes for 10,000 sites. Allowing room for expansion on each disc, these data are spread over seven separate discs. From these seven discs a series of other data discs are created – Period, Parish, etc. - which are used to generate catalogues. In total these secondary discs account for some eleven megabytes. The secondary discs rather than the site sequential discs are the ones more often used to abstract and transfer data to new discs, prior to producing a non-standard catalogue.

Because of the monopoly of our equipment by Sites and Monuments Record work, we are only now about to gain first hand experience of applying computers to excavation recording and processing. But since it has always been our intention to do this, we have for a long time been using record forms, designed as computer input forms, on all our excavations. So far we have thus enjoyed all the bureaucracy of form-filling without any of the benefits. Following the experience of the DOE Central Excavation Unit, applications will include error checking in recorded context relationships, and display (in catalogue form) of the overall structure of the site; the production of Finds Catalogues, as an aid to further analysis; catalogues containing all context data with summaries of artefacts, environmental material, and original record references (plans, photographs, etc.); separate index catalogues by each site record, type-object catalogues with appropriate cross references and indexes. There is no doubt that the use of a computer will be of much benefit both during the excavation and during post excavation work, both for analysis and in the creation of a structured, indexed and easily reproducible archive. From the excavation record files, summary data will automatically be abstracted to add to Sites and Monuments Record files. This facility is extremely valuable since it is inconceivable that even summary information on artefacts and contexts from all excavations could be integrated with a Sites and Monuments Record by any other means.

One area in which, as expected, we are finding the computer particularly useful is in the analysis and organisation of terms for classification and retrieval purposes. Many attempts have been made by individuals and committees in recent years to come to an agreement on terms to be used in Record Systems, invariably resulting in rather rigid structuring, catering neither for regional differences, nor individual preferences. The capacity of a computer to generate indexes and glossaries in any preferred combination seems to me to go a long way towards resolving such problems. In our case, though we employ in our Sites and Monuments Record controlled lists for some fields – such as Period, Form, History, or Status, no such control is exercised over, for example, Generic Site type, or Artefact types. We have always felt that pre-determined lists tend to inhibit retrieval, restricting the flexibility required, especially if such lists are used at a time when a whole new Sites and Monuments Record is being compiled. Our policy has been to use simple name terms wherever possible. In practice the terms used on input may be terms derived from the source record (e.g. O.S. Archaeology Division cards) or whatever the indexer considers appropriate. Alternative terms may be entered if required. Our Site Record also has a Keyword Field. Again the indexer determines the terms used. These may be simple terms, or alternative simple terms, or detailed terms. In the latter case this is generally a result of someone researching a particular site or type of site. The next stage is to generate periodically, by computer, lists of terms to see what is actually being used. Lists can also be automatically generated to discover how the terms used, for example, in Generic Type, relates to the Period classifications, or what kind of keywords are being used in relation to each site type.

As an index to the Record, such alphabetical lists may be reworked and used to provide a synonym list or, if required, a classified (i.e. hierarchical) list. The terms may also be arranged into categories, using other terms which are not necessarily used in the Record itself. With a small amount of effort therefore, terms used in the Record can be ordered in a variety of ways to suit individual retrieval requirements. It is left to the enquirer to persue such lists and decide for himself which terms are likely to encompass the subject of his enquiry. The advantage of using a computer in this way is that the index or indexes used as an initial guide to retrieval can be changed and reorganised from time to time without having to change the terms used in the actual Record, though on occasions it may be desirable to do this when existing terms are manifestly found to be incorrect (as a result of field survey) or become obsolete.

The manpower requirements for applying information technology to archaeological problems have not received much attention. I suspect that this is because much of this application is still on an experimental basis, or is still in the early stages of application as an established working practice, or is being used for a limited number of finite projects. But if micro-processor systems are to become an established part of working life in dealing with all aspects of archaeological information within an Archaeological Unit, then thought should be given as to who will conduct the operations, what degree of supervision will be necessary, and what degree of expertise in computer work is required.

How self-reliant should systems be? Is it necessary to have someone acting as a 'Data Manager'? If so, can we afford such a person, and can we pay enough to keep him or her? What skills and expertise will staff have to have, or acquire? What training will be necessary and how will this be achieved?

At present, a whole variety of ad hoc situations and arrangements exist. In our own case, whilst contributing to systems analysis, we have relied on the Central Excavation Unit for software development. The C.E.U's own expertise here is largely self acquired, supported by the expertise of people previously trained in computer work, engaged from time to time on a short-term basis. Our own operational experience is largely confined to one member of staff (our Records Officer) who is involved in sorting and processing work on a full-time basis, although at intervals a typist is employed to input data. Our present system of operations is thus very centralised: The Record Officer deals with all requests, is responsible for routine editing and processing and the adaptation and manipulation of existing software to suit our own particular needs. This has the advantage of maintaining consistency in data management, and the work is carried out much more quickly and efficiently than if individual members of staff were responsible for their own processing work. On the other hand, this does not provide much opportunity for staff to acquire computer experience (which is undoubtedly beneficial) and means placing heavy reliance on one person whose replacement would cause no small inconvenience.

A number of staff will want to use the smaller micro-computers we have recently acquired, and we many well look towards developing simpler interactive programs than we use at present. On the other hand is it better to employ one person, preferably a typist with archaeological knowledge, to input all data, say, on an excavation, rather than involve a whole range of people in this work? The amount of editing necessary to correct input errors may show which is best. Undoubtedly the picture will be very different in a few years' time, as present personnel acquire new skills and new personnel come into archaeology with a knowledge of computers acquired as a part of their normal education.

The euphoria and excitement with which we greet, and will continue to greet, the new technology should be tempered by the realisation that the sort of financial and organisational framework within which the majority of Archaeological Units operate may be the main constraint rather than the capacity of information technology itself. There is a world of difference between developing, testing and applying in a small way programs and systems which are undoubtedly *capable* of manipulating information to the required effect, and the full blown use of micro–computers as an integral part of information collection and management on a week in week out, year in year out basis. There is little experience of the application of information technology in a sustained way to regular working pratice, or of some of the practical problems that arise.

So, let us not assume that the purchase of a micro–computer will overnight, or even in the medium term, solve all our problems. Our own conclusion after nearly two years' experience, is that we need much *more* experience before we can best use 'IT' within the limitations imposed by organisation and funding. It may well be that our applications will of necessity have to be limited and that at present our sights are set too high.

Bibliography

Stewart, J.D. (ed) 1980 Micro–computers in archaeology *Museum Documentation Association Occasional Paper* 4. MDA, Duxford.

CHAPTER 6

THE IMPACT OF COMPUTERIZED INFORMATION SYSTEMS ON AMERICAN ARCHAEOLOGY: AN OVERVIEW OF THE PAST DECADE

Sylvia Gaines

Arizona State University

We are entering a new era and opportunities abound to exploit new technologies and as a consequence to explore new ideas and new concepts. We have the good fortune to be sitting at the beginning of what I believe is a new phase in archaeology.

When I was asked to speak on informtion retrieval in American archaeology, I was struck by the enormity of the task. Three million square miles of area of the U.S. poses a problem in even attempting to survey the vast array of research in the space of a single paper. However, what I want to describe is my impression of the trends and the directions in which American archaeology is evolving. I have chosen to present an overview of the past decade – an historical sketch as it were – to illustrate what I feel to be rather dramatic changes in methodological and technical capabilities which result from our coming of age in the computer era. To accomplish this I will draw heavily upon the work which has been in progress in the American Southwest and more specifically in Arizona over the last decade. In concluding my discussion I will give some projections on where we will be going in the current decade of the 1980s.

My home state of Arizona is a fascinating paradox of extremes. The federal landholding agencies control over 80 percent of the 114,000 square miles in the state. These acreages include those of the Forest Service, Bureau of Land Management, and many square miles of National parks and Monuments such as the Grand Canyon, not to mention a number of Indian reservations which includes the vast Hopi and Navajo lands. I would estimate that there are over 20,000 recorded prehistoric sites in the state most of which have not been excavated. It is fair to say that, in addition, many still remain unrecorded. Arizona has long enjoyed the reputation of being the nation's field laboratory for anthropology. Much of the information on this vast cultural resource resides in data bases in the 2 major state universities, the state museum and several private institutions. The state universities have also enjoyed one of the longest histories of computerized information retrieval in American archaeology. We have the environment necessary for future innovations in computer aided research and management of our cultural resources.

Electronic computers are having far reaching affects on society and archaeology, like many disciplines, is still experiencing the impact of this new technology. Historically, archaeology followed closely in the footsteps of the physical and natural sciences in exploiting the power of the computer in mathematical and statistical applications. If the 1960s was the Age of Computer Experimentation for archaeology, the 1970s was surely the Age of Computer Implementation. With the rapid extension and enhancements of applications perhaps the current decade, the 1980s, will be labelled the Age of Computer Exploitation.

The decade of the 70s saw the beginning of a variety of new approaches for archaeology. Archaeology had broken free from the earlier emulation of the physical sciences in relying on their software development, just as it, a decade even earlier in the 60s had broken forth from time/space systematics and began to focus on more complex questions of behavioral systems. Computer applications were beginning to be incorporated into research designs for data analysis and data management.

Archaeology has always been burdened with the difficulties of archiving and indexing cultural material. The seventies saw a veritable explosion in the amount of information. The existing manual techniques of maintaining collections of documents and information were becoming unwieldy and the ennui of manual searching limited the usefulness in research. Fortunately, concurrent with the proliferation of data capture in the field, computer technology began to provide the tools to automate the indexing of much of this information and new methods of managing the rapidly growing data base. Archaeologists began to experiment with computer based files.

This early phase in the evolution of automated data management is reflected in the focus of the conferences held during this interim. Meetings such as the one held in 1972 at the University of Arkansas (Chenhall 1981:1) was concerned with topics such as – what data should be stored? Participants of this conference concurred that automation of archaeological data was probably a good thing but any agreement on common data categories was far from realised. By the end of the decade, conferences and symposia, especially at the national and international level, had evolved to quite a different tone. Enough experimentation had taken place to allow us to identify weaknesses in our approach as well as to demonstrate the strengths in those applications which proved successful. Concern with data requirements, nuts and bolts of hardware and software, were put aside, and quite rightly so. Most archaeologists by the end of the decade were convinced that computer use was here to stay and that the goal was how to make the most of the potential.

Principle forces behind this rapidly advancing trend toward automation need to be addressed before we turn to the impact of the seventies on American archaeology. I see three main concurrent elements as contributing to the increased use of information systems in the United States:

1) change in our theoretical focus,
2) the rise of Cultural Resource Management
3) the availability of computer hardware and software.

The first concerns a change in focus in the theoretical and methodological interests of archaeologists. Although it is beyond the scope of this discussion to explore the historical background of this "new" archaeology which began in the 1960s, the direction which it took was not only amenable to, but in many instances required computer methodology. Time-space systematics were put aside for theory-based questions about economics, environments and social organization requiring systematic analysis of a variety of data and elaborate modelling. The normative view of a single, large site providing the needed information, gave way to regional analyses incorporating both large and small sites in order to answer questions about population size, structure and distribution, and articulation with the environment. Micro-economic models came into vogue as well as probability sampling strategies which allowed for statistical predictability of our survey data. Indeed, as one colleague phrased it, statistics became the bandwagon leading the pack (Thomas 1978:235). These research directions were enhanced by and even required a computerized information system for both the management and analyses of the ever increasing data base.

The second phenomenon had its beginning in the salvage archaeology of the 1930s but did not reach its full impact on archaeology until the past decade. I refer to the rise of Cultural Resource Management – what we term CRM. In the late 1960s and early 1970s a number of federal legislative acts laid the framework for this acceleration. Most notable was the National Environmental Protection Act which required preparation of environmental impact statements prior to any impact on federal lands; and secondly, the National Historic Preservation Act which provided guidelines for data recovery and the national registry of sites. "The legislation has also included authorization for the expenditure of federal funds to carry out archaeological work as a part of the mitigation of the impact on cultural resources of federally funded or licensed projects that involve disturbance of the earth's surface" (Scholtz and Million 1981: 15)

I cite the CRM examples only to show that archaeological investigations were being regarded as necessary and adequate funds were being provided. What did this mean in terms of computer utilization? First, the CRM data management requirements literally exploded during the 70s. National economic expansion saw major efforts in roads, pipelines, mining and urban development of all types – many of which required archaeological investigations.

Universities and their cadres of trained archaeology students were the first to meet the CRM challenge. If you consider the background for this trend, the focus of archaeological theory, coupled with the increasing use of computer facilities, it is no wonder that implementation of automated site files for CRM inventory control and research sprang up rapidly. The need for initial planning and on-going management of archaeological data required easy and rapid access.

Automated site inventories have grown extensively in universities, state and federal agencies, and more recently in the private sector. Using the state of Arizona as an example, in the early 70s only the two larger universities, Arizona State and the University of Arizona, had employed computerized information systems for CRM. CRM work under the auspices of the universities was often justified not simply as an economic venture, but rather on the research and training function that it provided. Both the US Forest Service and Bureau of Land Management contracted for much of their CRM work through these universities as did the Corps of Engineers and the Bureau of Reclamation. However, by the late 70s a score of private companies, both large and small had joined the CRM bandwagon. The larger ones, often based in other states, had their own computer information systems, and even micro-computer facilities in each office. CRM work in the private sector was strictly an economic venture. This profit vis-a-vis research objective is hotly debated in archaeology today. As a result of these 2 disparate goals, a number of computer files are currently operative in Arizona alone. What this means in terms of compatability of automated information will be discussed later.

The third factor contributing to expansion of information systems relates to the availability of hardware and software and to the cost effectiveness of data processing in general. By the early 1970s all major institutions and many smaller colleges had acquired some type of computer facility for academic use. Availability for archaeological use varied as widely then as it does today. Some institutions provide unlimited use and researchers are not changed. Only funded projects are required to contribute a portion of their budget if data processing is involved. The major trends in processing centred on time sharing and access via terminals. The evolution of computer facilities and archaeological use at Arizona State University is typical of many across the nation. Prior to the 70s several different facilities existed on my campus. In the early 70s the computing facilities were integrated and a large mainframe, UNIVAC 1110, was installed. In turn, it too was replaced by an AMDAHL 470 in the late 1970s; in addition to 5 mini PDP 11/70s were added. The latter are located at various remote processing sites throughout the campus to provide the terminal interface. The Engineering College has installed a large Honeywell MULTICS system this past year and this semester the AMDAHL 470 is being upgraded to an IBM 3081. Archaeologists may access the campus computers in any of the remote sites on campus or by terminals in the Anthropology Building. As one might gather the Arizona State University campus is quite extensive and the current enrollment is approximately 41,000 students.

Coupled with the growth in computer facilities is the dramatic reduction in data processing and storage costs. For storage costs alone, a 2 to 1 reduction every three years has been the trend. On our newest computer the cost of storing on disk 3200 site records is only $32. Not only have break-through in costs, size and speed aided archaeological work but the availability of software and friendlier user interfaces have also greatly enhanced usability. Historically, archaeologists have not been software experts, and frequently programs that have been developed for archaeologists usually have been for projects or specific applications. The cost of developing software has dictated that we rely on general management or statistical programs for most of our applications. This situation is generally true of most archaeology departments in universities and it is no different at ASU. The nearly universal broad-based packages, such as SPSS, SAS, etc., met our early needs. During the 70s user interfaces became simplified and many of the existing program packages were upgraded and enhanced so that archaeological requirements continued to be supported, if not ideally satisfied. We are still a long way from archaeological problem orientated languages and application programs.

Let me turn now to some of the more prominent applications which have been developed during the last 10 years in the United States. I would like to distinguish between management of information and research and analysis. Although these functions need not be mutually exclusive, the majority of application emphasize either one or the other.

Probably hundreds of data-bases relating to detailed artefact analyses have sprung up in the major institutions. These are what I consider 'personal computerized archives' directed toward a specific, often short termed goal. What I will discuss rather, are the more permanent, long term data bases, both analytical and management orientated. By far the majority of management data-bases are directly related to CRM inventory control functions. Research data-bases often do not contain the types of managment infomation necessary for inventory control. Conversely, an automated data-base designed for inventory management will contain different data categories than one designed for fine grained research analyses.

During the 1970s a number of federal agencies involved in cultural resource management began to design and develop automated inventory files. The U.S. Forest Service, one of the largest of the land holding agencies, was probably the leader in this respect. The Forest Service has management responsibility for approximately 187 million acres of land in the United States. Forest Service personnel estimate that 3 to 5 million cultural resources (sites) both historic and prehistoric exist on this acreage (Green 1980). Rather than attempt a single master file (data) for all sites and all sites information, the Forest Service adopted a regional approach which decentralized the data and made it available through different data-bases which are specific to the various regions. Consideration was given to integrating regional files with Forest Service general information management systen known as System 2000. This system in turn is tied to the general land managment planning effort of the Forest Service. It allows the mapping of archaeological resources in conjunction with environmental variables which can provide insights for both research and planning. The Southwest region of the Forest Service, in which Arizona is located, has been a leader in this endeavour and my institution has worked closely with Forest Service personnel to assure understanding of objectives.

An example from the National Park Service illustrates an innovative approach to an automated information system. This data-base project, sponsored by the Dept. of Interior, was charged with the task of compiling information to assess potential impacts to an area rich in uranium in the northwestern part of the state of New Mexico. Over 31,000 site records, derived from a wide variety of sources, have been entered into the data-base, covering an areal extent of 142,000 hectares. An interactive program was developed for the National Park Service which allows direct inquiry to the data-base via terminals. To date eight terminals have been placed in various agency offices throughout that region. Requested information may include the type and location of all sites and surveys, bibliographic references, the year and the institution responsible for the work as well as other pertinent archaeological data. In addition, distributional maps are produced from a graphics terminal at the home office. These maps are of immeasurable value in the early planning of earth modifying activities and in the preparation of environmental impact statements. One interesting aspect of this project is that data were derived from so many disparate sources – federal, state, museum, institutions and the private sector. This data sharing concept will be elaborated upon later but this degree of cooperation between multiple agencies is worth noting.

Turning to state sponsored automated data-bases, we look mainly at state museums and universities. By far the majority of these instututions throughout the U.S. still maintain only manual files systems, but during the past decade, about a dozen states began to automate archaeological informtion. Arizona is typical of such an endeavour and has provided a model for state institutions and agencies considering computerization of such projects. Of the two major museums located in the state, only Arizona State Museum has developed an automated system. The other museum, a large private research institution, although active in CRM work, relies on a manual system as well as contracting outside for data processing. Again, these data-bases within this state alone, constitute information on thousands of archaeological sites and are mainly for inventory control purposes. However, at Arizona State University we have attempted to incorporate data categories required for a number of research questions, particularly questions relating to demographic, organizational and environmental factors.

Up to this point I have been discussing management oriented data-bases. However, research functions have played an important role in automated data-bases developed in the past decade. This type of data-base use largely resides within major institutions or among a number of researchers who share a common research goal. Three of the better known research applications which I will discuss breifly are the Koster Project information system, the ADAM system for remote field work, and the Southwestern Anthropological Research Group.

The Koster Project began the development of a computer data processing and retrieval system in 1972, the purpose of which was to facilitate the archaeological investigation at the large Koster site located in west central Illinois. This system provided basic support to a complex, multidisciplinary research project by processing information for a large scale excavation of the deeply stratified Koster site (Brown et al 1981:67). The CDC 6400 computer facility at Northwestern University was time-shared by remote terminal connection from the site. Programs were written in APL which accomplished high priority data processing tasks needed to resolve field stratigraphic problems as well as to organize materials for specialized laboratory analysis. Two file types were used – data files and indices to the data files. Both were structured by provenience unit (Brown et al 1981:78-79).

Turning to the second example of a research application, the ADAM project is somewhat unique. It was one of the first attempts to take the computer capability into the field to aid research at a remote location. In 1971, the project on the Navajo Indian Reservation at White Goat Ruin in northeastern Arizona was undertaken to determine what effect rapid feedback of computer analyses would have on an excavation and survey (Gaines and Gaines 1980:467; Gaines 1971a; 1971b:7-8; 1972:40-70; 1974:454-461; 1977:59-77). Access to the Arizona State University computer facility was accomplished via time sharing terminal located at the site. Turn-around time from field data recovery, through laboratory analyses, to data entry, and to the final computer report, was in the order of 24 hours. This response time was rapid enough to aid in tactical field decisions on a daily basis. The ADAM system software was written from scratch since no adequate time-sharing data management and analysis was available at the time. Although crude by todays standards, the ADAM project demonstrated not only the feasibility, but the practicality of such an advanced application and served as a model for later work.

The third example of a well known automated research file is provided by the Southwestern Anthropological Research Group [SARG], a project in which I have been involved for the past dozen years. SARG was founded in 1971 as a cooperative effort of a number of Southwestern archaeologists interested in devoting a portion of their individual research to problems of broad cultural significance. For the past 10 years we have been collecting survey data in a standardized format and storing these in a common computerized data base at Arizona State University. These data are used to address questions relating to basic behavioural processes. At the outset, we agreed to focus on matters of settlement patterning in the prehistoric Southwest (Gaines and Plog 1980:1). This volunteer organization is composed of approximately 20 researchers who are located in institutions and agencies throughout the country, but whose main field work centres in the American Southwest (Arizona, New Mexico, and Utah).

It was recognized at the onset that through time the research focus would require modification. Computer methodology was designed with this type of evolution in mind and the data format and processing procedures were established so that these could serve as a basis for a flexible and expanding system for storing and manipulating data (Gaines 1978:121). The data-base has been operational since 1975 and it has been possible to test the concept and implementation in actual practice. This early data-base included a maximum of 135 variables per site and eight projects had been entered, totalling 2500 sites.

During the past several years the SARG data-base has undergone major revisions resulting in the redefinition of some data and reduction of the total number of variables to 74. These data reflect categories of location, site characteristics and environment. The availability of the data in computer format alllowed the reduction and restructuring of the previously entered data automatically and required little or no additional effort on the part of the participants. To date there are 3 new projects, with the total data-base numbering over 3500 sites. In summary, flexibility was a cornerstone which provided a basis for data extension.

Due to lack of research funding in the initial stages SARG was launched using readily available software. These standard packages provided both data management and analytical functions. Several previously developed systems could have been adapted but considerable time and money would have been required to adequately modify these systems to satisfy both the management and manipulatory requirements. The same situation would have been true if a totally new system was developed specifically for SARG use. Given these contraints it was decided to explore the feasibility of utilizing a programming package already maintained on the computer at ASU, namely the Statistical Package for the Social Sciences (SPSS). While most archaeologists are familiar with the mathematical and statistical functions of SPSS, the programs capability for handling large quantities of data and general data-base management tasks had not been widely explored, at least, not in 1973 (Gaines 1978:121-123).

In addition to the afore-mentioned software there were two unique data management packages written in the 70s on which I would like to comment briefly. SELGEM (SELf-GEnerating Master), a program package developed at the Smithsonian, is used widely among American museums today (Rieger 1981:32). SELGEM has undergone a number of enhancements since early 1970 which makes it more amendable to archaeological data. Furthermore, it is written in COBOL, a language found almost universally on all large computers.

GRIPHOS (General Retrieval and Information Processing for the Humanities Oriented Studies) is another museum program package developed in the early 1970s by the Museum Computer Network, a consortium of museums in the New York area. Several state museums, notably Arkansas and Florida, have adopted GRIPHOS as their data-base management system for archaeological work. However, the programs are in PL/1, which has limited their use.

Other than the museum oriented SELGEM system there is little agreement or correspondence on program packages and language use in American archaeology. This has been the status throughout the past decade and there is little anticipation of change in the near future. Archaeologists generally rely on software supported by their institution or agency and are just not given to writing their own programs – either for management or analaysis. However, as languages and user interfaces evolve into more user freindly realms, hopefully archaeological oriented application programs will be forthcoming.

What have been the effects of computerized information retrieval on archaeology? Clearly, a number of changes have resulted and while some are evident others are more difficult to separate from directional changes in our theoretical and methodological preceptions. Fortunately there has been a gradual maturing of knowledge about how to effectively use computers in archaeological work (Chenhall 1981:2). The early "wait and see" attitude of the past decade has given way to more positive views. Applications of information retrieval which have demonstrated usefulness and cost effectiveness, as well as the increasing availability of hardware and software, have aided in this change of attitude.

Certainly a major impact on the 70s concerns the number of archaeologists both professional and students, who became involved, or at least knowledgeable, in archaeological automated systems. The growing need for expertise resulted in curriculum changes. In some cases formal classes were added to archaeology departments rather than relying on mathematics, engineering and computer science for training students. Students throughout the country began to realize that potential jobs often required such training and individuals with this background grew in demand. Early in the 70s Arizona State University was one of the few institutions offering such courses. By the close of the decade anthropology departments were slowly beginning to offer their own classes in computer topics as well as in quantitative methods. ASU is quite exceptional in that we now offer 4 courses of this nature.

The impact of expanded hardware and software capabilities on archaeological applications in the past decade was most dramatic. Wider selection of size as well as lower processing and storage costs were critical factors. American archaeologists are almost totally dependant on computer facilities of their institution or agency. Although the range of facilities varied considerably from one institution to another, the decade saw a gradual increase in the number and power of computer resources available. Again, ASU is typical of many state schools. As discussed earlier, both mainframe and minis were upgraded. Remote processing sites sprang up over the campus and most departments added CRT terminals for their in-house use. Archaeology was no exception. We upgraded our terminals and continually requested additional mainframe disk storage for our ever increasing database of archaeological information. Graphics terminals and software were in increased demand, not only in archaeology, but in other disciplines as well. The university maintains a graphics remote processing facility, with a full array of digitizers and plotters.

Another impact of automated information systems concerns the increased need for clarity and precision in terms of data and procedures. Where gross levels of precision and implicity had been adequate, definitions now had to be complete and consistant; operations had to be precisely specified and the logic of the algorithm had to be explicit and unambigiously stated. Consistency in data definitions is critical when a number of researchers are involved in data capture for a common project; especially when data is destined for complex statistical analyses. These factors are forcing the archaeologist into a new mode of thinking.

During the 70s archaeologists involved in computerised projects often resorted to standardized recording forms for field and lab use, to assure as much quality control as possible. The recording forms of the 70s ranged from 'fill in the box with the correct code' to simply spaces for free text associated with specific data categories. Later, mark sense and optical character reader forms became more popular, all with the eye toward precision or at least standardization. The utility of dictionaries and thesauruses became realised at this juncture.

Certainly the change in focus in our theoretical concerns has lead us into new data types and categories. The management and analyses of these data would have been cumbersome, if not impossible, without computer resources. For example, spatial and locational analyses were incorporated into many research projects in the 1970s. In the early part of the decade, site locations were generally recorded in longitude and latitude. As computer routines and mapping programs for spatial patterns became more available, for example, the SYMAP and GIPSY programs, archaeologists recognized that site loations recorded as UTM coordinates would be of much more utility. As a result many archaeologists are now recording locational data in metric.

Another important aspect is the concept of data sharing or resource sharing. Although this type of utilization is still in its infancy, several successful examples serve as models for continual growth of this approach. One such example, referred to earlier in this paper, is the SARG organization which developed in the early 70s to facilitate cooperative research in the American Southwest. Members of the SARG organisation feel strongly that sharing pooled data on a single computer facility has opened up new avenues for research. The SARG example has attracted wide interest in both the U.S. and abroad. Since SARG participants are involved on only a part time basis, results are not produced as quickly or as in as great a quantity as in other approaches. However, it does have the advantage of being far less expensive and results in an extensive data-base adequate to address regional questions.

SARG represents an application which involves most of the dimensions and problems of management and creation of a large data-base of survey information. The cooperative structure and organisation of SARG is unique at least in American archaeology, and the voluntary nature of the group in terms of time and effort places constraints on the research design (Gaines and Gaines 1981: Dean 1978:103). This past decade has been considerable evolution in SARG in terms of hardware availaibility, user interface and research focus. Although the results of our approach must await final evaluation, several broad contributions of this data sharing appliations have been identified:

Our site recording format which was initiated in 1971, not only served to structure the SARG data but has had impact outside the organisation. The current high standards and more complete observations which generally characterize Southwestern archaeological survey are probably due largely to the SARG survey format (Gaines and Plog 1980:3). In this respect, SARG has served as a model for a number of other institutions and agencies involved in similar efforts.

Another contribution relates to the potential size of the pooled data-base. There are approximately 20,000 sites which are potential candidates for entry into the data-base. Given the level of archaeological work in the Southwest, information on several thousand additional sites per year could be incorporated into SARG making it a data-base unparalleled in extent and sophistication for research purposes (Gaines and Plog 1980:3).

The utilization of a common data-base on a single computer, accessible to participants who are located throughout the contry offers substantial advantages in terms of standardization, processing costs and availability. This type of resource sharing is still unique to American archaeology but its potential is being explored in the SARG research effort.

Other data sharing examples are found in the large federal agencies such as the Bureau of Land Management (BLM) and U.S. Forest Service which have been compiling inventory control files. Although only a portion of these files have been automated, these data-bases may be accessed by authorized archaeologists. Organisations at the state level are becoming more aware of and concerned with the concept of data sharing. In both Arizona and New Mexico, for example, committees have been established to idetify both automated and manual data-base needs and functions required of agencies involved in archaeological data gathering. With multiple data-bases in existence within these states today, much redundancy and inefficiency results. Clearly the ultimate goal is to maximize standar-disation to facilitate data sharing.

Left to the normal course of events the acceptance of a greater degree of standardisation would be slow at best. As an example, I cite a 1977 conference on CRM data-bases which was held to explore this issue.

Participants included both federal and state agencies which were actively involved in archaeological data management. All agreed on the potential economic benefits of standardization in terms of time, cost and elimination of redundancy. However, after examining the data categories being recorded by participating agencies, it was concluded that only five data elements were common to all of the data sets (site designation, location, county, recording institution and whether artifact collections had been made). Current CRM demands may portend increasing federal pressure for standardization. This fact, combined with the economic incentives, should accelerate the trend.

I would like to conclude by briefly examining the future of some of the issues which I have explored in this discussion. No one would deny that a greater variety of hardware and software will be more available in the future as processing and storage costs are dramatically decreased. Items such as forms control terminals and portable data recorders will greatly enhance our data entry and verification procedures (Gaines and Gaines 1980:466-468). However, the human factor will remain the expensive item. If this trend is toward greater cost effectiveness and availability, we must constantly guard against becoming so locked into or so committed to one system, one language, one application that we actually retrogress in terms of potentials. Flexibility must be the cornerstone of today's applications. Data-bases are like cultural episodes – they come into being, flourish, decline or become obsolete. As technologies and research foci change, we must retain a degree of flexibility in order to make full use of the automated potential of information systems.

One of our major problems concerns the current debate on the question of standardization and comparability. Advocates of comparability hold that it must be achieved at the level of inference and test results, and not at the observational level. Those in the opposite camp, argue that standardization is the starting point and comparability cannot be achieved without this control. I think that this issue will ultimately be resolved. Both state and federal agencies could begin by providing archaeologists with better guidelines for data capture, quality, procedural and organizational controls.

Clearly the growth potential and enhancements of our automated information systems is tied directly to the economic conditions. American archaeologists have already felt the cut back of traditional funding sources, such as the National Science Foundation. With stiff competition for scarce funding, perhaps we will see an increase in data and resource sharing ventures.

The ever increasing human impact on the environment, which includes both historic and prehistoric sites, is of deep concern to American archaeologists. Even with strict environmental laws and stringent guidelines regarding data recovery, the archaeological record is rapidly being destroyed. It is fair to say that ultimately we will reach the point when most of our data will reside in computerized data-bases – rather than in the ground. Today we must be concerned with not only the current but also the future benefits of computerized data-bases and attempt to include as much relevant information as possible. Obviously the economics of today will determine the level of specificity and utility of tomorrow's computerized information systems.

Addendum

Since the Spring of 1982 when this paper was presented, there has been a rapid infusion of microcomputers into American archaeology. This new capability is replacing many of the earlier mainframe orientated tasks, from simple statistical analyses to complex data management. The micro-computer trend will continue to grow until virtually all types of archaeolo-gical endeavours are utilising this capability.

Bibliography

Brown, James A. *et al* 1981 The Koster Project information retrieval application. In: *Data bank Applications in Archaeology.* S. W. Gaines (Ed) University of Arizona Press. Tuscon.
Chenhall, Robert G. 1981 Computerized data bank management. In: *Data bank Applications in Archaeology.* S. W. Gaines (Ed.) University of Arizona Press. Tuscon.
Dean, Jeffrey S. 1978 An evaluation of the initial SARG research design. In: *Investigation of the Southwestern Anthropological Research Group:* An experiment in Archaeological Cooperation. R. C. Euler and G. J. Gumerman (Eds.) Museum of Northern Arizona. Flagstaff.
Gaines, Sylvia W. 1971a. Computer application in a field situation *Newsletter of Computer Archaeology.* Vol VII, No. 1 Arizona State University. Tempe.
Gaines, Sylvia W. 1971b. Computer utilization for archaeological field problems. *Science and Archaeology.* 8.
Gaines, Sylvia W. 1974 Computer aided decision – making procedures for archaeologial field problems. *American Antiquity* 39 (3).
Gaines, Sylvia W. 1977 Interactive data retrieval for archaeological field problems. In: *Revista Mexicana de Estudios Antropologicos.* Tomo XXII:I Mexico City.
Gaines, Sylvia W. 1978 Computer applications of SARG data. In: *Investigations of the Southwestern Anthropological Research Group.* R. C. Euler and G. J. Gumerman (Eds.) Museum of Northern Arizona. Flagstaff.
Gaines, Sylvia W. 1971–79 *Newsletter of Computer Archaeology* – Editor. Arizona State University. Tempe.
Gaines, Sylvia W. and Warren M. Gaines 1980 Future trends in computer applications. *American Antiquity* 45 (3).
Gaines, Sylvia W. and Warren M. Gaines 1981 What future data-bases have to offer archaeology. In: *Proceedings of the X Congress*: Untion Internacional de Ciencias Prehistoricas y Protohistoricas. Mexico City.
Gaines, Sylvia W. and Fred Plog 1980 *Continuing Research of the Southwestern Anthropological Research Group.* Proposal submitted to National Science founda-tion. Grant No. BNS 80-04571. Washington.
Gaines, Sylvia (with James Schoenwetter and Donald Weaver) 1973 *Definition and*

preliminary study of the Midevale Site. Anthropological Research paper #6. Department of Anthropology. Arizona State University. Tempe.

Green, Dee F. 1980 *Approaches to mass archaeological data storage: the USDA Forest Service System.* Paper presented at the 1980 meeting of the Society of American Archaeology. Philadelphia.

Rieger, Anne 1981 AZ SITE: The Arizona State Museum site survey data-base. In: *Data Bank Applications in Archaeology.* S. W. Gains (Ed.) University of Arizona

Scholtz, Sandra and Michael Million 1981 A management information system for archaeological resources. In: *Data Bank Applications in Archaeology.* S. W. Gaines (Ed,) University of Arizona Press. Tuscon.

Thomas, David H. 1978 The awful truth about statistics. *American Antiquity.* 43(2).

CHAPTER 7

MUSEUMS – 'CABINETS OF CURIOSITIES' OR CENTRES OF INFORMATION?

Jennifer Stewart

Museum Documentation Association

Museums are usually viewed either as 'cabinets of curiosities' or less frequently, as centres of information (Flood, 1982). Before looking at these views it would be worthwhile to review computerised archaeology briefly, and one particular aspect, information systems in archaeology.

Information Technology and Information Systems are the main topics of this conference. What is meant by 'information technology'; what are 'information systems', and do we really have such systems in archaeology today? 'Information technology' as a term has slowly crept into the consciousness of post-industrial Britain, and various papers have attempted to define it (Fagg, 1981; Nora and Minc, 1980), and the implications of adopting new technology in a variety of fields (G.B., 1981 a and b; Higgins, 1981; Lane, 1981). A definition has been produced for Information Technology Year (Inform, 1982):

> 'the acquisition, processing, storage and dissemination of vocal, pictorial, textual and numeric information using a micro-electronics based combination of computing and telecommunications'.

This paper is restricted to a discussion of computerised information retrieval of (museum) records.

Most people will not be convinced we have information systems in British archaeology. 'Information systems' implies a comprehensive theoretical and practical framework for the 'archaeological archive' from site to museum. This we do *not* have in Britain at the moment (Stewart, 1980a). The archaeologist in the field or site-hut is busy gathering data on data-sheets or microcomputers; the curator in the museum is recording some of that information for later processing; the postgraduate then re-records some of that re-recorded information for his/her thesis. A case of re-inventing the wheel several times? While specific computerisation projects require separate, detailed and individual recording, it would be desirable to make this information more readily available and to avoid duplication of effort. A core of information is common to all three above examples, such as site name, object name, material, small find number etc. While some would say it is impossible to get agreement on all categories of information to be useful for both the site and the museum, it should be possible to reach some form of agreement on these common areas of information. The storage, structure and content of archaeological archives have been described elsewhere and will not be discussed further here (A.M.B., 1978; B.L.R&D., 1977; CBA, 1978; Graham, 1981; Michelmore, 1981; Museum of London, 1980; Rhodes, 1980; Scholtz and Chenhall, 1976; Stewart, 1980a, 1980d).

Computer applications in archaeology at the present have tended to concentrate on the development of one-off solutions for particular archaeological problems, as in graphics and statistical work. Current work in the field is described in *Computer Applications in Archaeology* and *Science and Archaeology,* and in various reviews in the late 1960's and early 1970's by Cowgill (1967); Whallon (1972) and Wilcock (1973). Gaines (1980) provides a look for the future, while Scollar (1982) gives a useful summary of the last thirty years of computer archaeology.

It would seem likely with the advent of cheap, powerful and generally available microcomputers, and enhanced data transfer and telecommunications facilities, that future applications will concentrate more on a communal approach to computerised data, rather than one-off projects. Such work may investigate data-bases, and the transfer of computerised records from one application or system to another through a variety of bridging mechanisms.

'Data-bases' and 'data banks' are notoriously misused terms. For the purposes of this chapter, Atkinson's (1979:51) definition of data-bases is used:

'a large collection of data (from 10/5 to 10/10 bytes) which is used for a number of purposes or by a number of people and which is supported by one or more computers.'

Bibliographic data-bases, such as IRAS and FRANCIS are two such examples, as is the data-base of C14 dates at the Institute of Archaeology (Moffat and Webb 1982). The term 'data-banks' appears to have been used in the past for a variety of manual and computerised applications. Both terms are defined by Oppenheim in this volume.

Within the three types of data models for data-base systems described by Date (1977) of hierarchical, network and relational types, the relational model may prove the more popular for future work. A survey of databases of archaeological material is given in Lagrande (1978), others described in the literature include those in Hungary (Bezeczky, 1981); France (Le Maitre, 1978); and Japan (Oikawa, 1981).

Bridging mechanisms assist the transfer of data from one system to another. Not only technical aspects (file and directory formatting; choice of physical medium; coding of fields) but also theoretical aspects (an agreed 'core' of recording categories and analysis of text) are concerned. In addition, 'networking', means whereby machines can 'talk' to each other is involved.

Museums' interest in computerised archaeology is concerned not only with using computer equipment to document current accessions, but also as the recipients of excavation material – the finds and paper archive. In the future museums will have to cope with not only conventional site note-books but also with diskettes, computer stationery, tape cassette record-ings, microforms (including fiche) and videodiscs. The finds archive is however emasculated without a 'working' system of retrieving informa-tion – working in the sense that it answers both excavators' and museum queries. Hence museum interest in the 'pooling' of computerised excavation records if they exist, using data-base management systems or bridging mechanisms.

The Role of museums

The traditional view of museums is that a cabinet of curiosities, the closet of rarities where the precious and curious of the natural and the manmade world vie with each other for prominence and space. Ole Worms' seven-teenth century Copenhagen museum (Piggot, 1976: 103 and figure 11) and Bullock's museum in the centre of early Victorian London (Hancock, 1980, fig 71–72) typify such museums. Several authors have described the antiquarian scholarship which formed the background to these collections and the development of early museums (Piggot, 1976; Wittlin, 1970; Clarke, 1978).

The association of overstuffed basements and dusty displays lingers on. Even today, to call something 'a museum piece' is a term of derision.

However museums already act as a source of information by housing environmental records, more usually locality records about the natural and manmade environment as in Sites and Monuments Records (SMR's) (RCHM, 1978); biological and botanical records (Flood and Perring, 1978) geology sites (Cooper, 1981) and records for historical and industrial buildings. A review of museums as environmental record centres is provided in two recent publications (Stewart, 1980b and c).

The obvious extension of holding records and items about the surround-ing countryside is to explain or 'interpret' the environment for the public. Museums are not islands in space; they have to be considered in the context of life outside their walls, (Wittlin, 1970: 204). This interpretation can be effectively achieved in a multi-disciplinary basis within a set locality. The National Museum of Wales has been organising, for several years, public excursions to areas of interest in Wales, combining industrial archaeology and the natural sciences, expecially geology and botany (Sharpe and Howe, 1982).

The third example of museums as centres of information is in their vital role as the link between the public – those who pay for museums by rates or taxes, and the archaeologists – those who, through excavation, provide the collections for the museum. This important link, provided by museums, between the public and the archaeologists is one of the important themes of this conference.

Museums can help the archaeologist and the public make the fullest and most efficient use of our common heritage in museum collections, using the tools of information technology. One such example is where museums use computers not only for documentation but other aspects in the care and maintenance of public museum collections, for example, to monitor air conditioning, security, climatology and public enquiries. This is now being carried out at various museums around the world (Technology and Conservation, 1978, 1979, 1980; Museum, 1978).

Museums' role as centres of information will depend ultimately on museums knowing the range and size of their collections. Without an accurate knowledge of their holdings museums cannot carry out their main tasks of care and maintenance of collections within their custody; and to make these available to the public and researchers through displays and catalogues. Nearly thirty years ago, Atkinson called for co-operation in a national index of archaeological collections (Atkinson, 1955). He pointed out that it was little short of ridiculous that one was forced into an inordinately lengthy and tedious search in order to carry out archaeological research, due to lack of proper documentation.

The work of the Museum Documentation Association

Accurate knowledge of collections depends primarily on good documentation. Documentation can be defined here as the totality of information about items in collections; ways of retrieving that information; and more importantly, the uses to which one puts that retrieved information. Documentation encompasses both theoretical and practical parts of record-keeping.

Increasingly over the last few years, the work of the MDA has been concentrated on a total, and articulated, framework for the documenting of collections which would cover the theory and practicalities of cataloguing and inventory control. While this is called the Museum Documentation System it could apply to any institution with collections, such as archaeological units, Public Records Offices, archives, or Sites and Monuments

Figure 2 illustrates the various theoretical and practical component parts of the MDS. Each of these parts is described in the 'Guide to the Museum Documentation Systems' (MDA, 1982). An institution can adopt one or

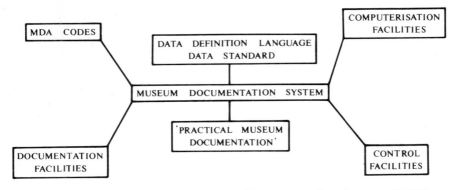

Fig. 2 Components of the Museum Documentation System (MDS).

more parts of the system when documenting its collections.

Help from the MDA covers two main areas, advisory services and computing facilities, both of which can be used by archaeologists, whether attached to a museum or not.

Advisory Services

The MDA can provide advice on the compatibility of a manual or computerised excavation archive with existing museum documentation systems. In addition advice on the feasibility of data transfer and interchange between microcomputer based systems of recording – 'dig' to 'dig', or 'dig' to museum, will be forthcoming in the future. MDA has already laid the basis of this work by investigating the exchange of museum records on magnetic tape (Light and Roberts, 1982) and also current computerisation facilities used in British museums as part of a project for CIDOC, the Documentation Committee of ICOM (UNESCO) (Roberts, 1982).

The MDA has set up and maintains a list of museums in Britain, with an agreed referencing code for each. A combination of the code and the object's identity number provides a unique identifier for each record, for use when combining records from more than one institution (MDA, 1979; MDA, 1982:37).

Computerisation facilities

Institutions wishing to computerise their collections have a choice of facilities from the MDA, depending on their needs and finances. These facilities range from a bureau service to undertake all stages of computerisation through to the acquisition of the MDA program package, GOS, to use on the institution's own computer. Future work will concentrate on providing GOS on a microcomputer which then could be used for a range of collections management tasks, including item documentation and inventory procedures (Light, 1982).

Card of

IDENTIFICATION

File		Institution	Council for Deserted Villages [D]
Filing number	ST 49 SE14	Locality number	L61 Part [D]
Locality name	St. Keyne's Chapel & Runston		[D]
Parish	Mathern district county region		[D]
Other geopolitical division			[D]
		Status : date **Ancient Mon.** [D]	Vice-county [D]
NGR	ST 49529160 accuracy	Map number [D]	Altitude [D]
Field recorder : date	**Jones, N.:1974=1976**		[D]
Museum recorder : date	**Roberts, D.A.:1/9/1976**		[D]
		Record type : method	[D]

DESCRIPTION

Type of locality	chapel & deserted village	[D]
	Condition of locality : date overgrown:1975	[D]
Shape **rectangle**	length **20m** width **5m(max)** height **7m(belfry)** depth area	[D]
General description of locality	chapel at Runston deserted medieval village dedicated to St. Keyne; late Norman date	[D]
Part : interest : description of interest **:period:(late) Norman**	cross reference	[D]

PRODUCTION

Method	person's role	name : date **:(late) Norman**	[D]

LOCALITY
A5 MUSEUM SUMMARY (1977-78)

MANAGE-MENT	Planning authority : planning status [D]	Conservation status : date [D] **Ancient Monument**
[C]	Management body [D]	Tenant/occupier [D]
ACCESS	Owner [D]	Development rights owner [D]
	Restrictions [D]	Category [D]
[C]	Approach route [D] turn north off A48 at Crick (ST481906) on B4571; park at brow of hill	
USE	Facilities [D] none	
	Present use [D] agriculture (pasture)	
	Potential use [D] educational (O level, A level, university extra mural)	
[C]	Threats to locality [D] none	next appraisal date [D] June 1978
PEOPLE	Visit reason [D] survey	Visitor : date name : date Interested person role [D] Cardiff University Dept. Extra Mural Studies: 1974-1976
[C]	Map or plan — date : publisher : sheet : scale : note [D] 1975: : :1m to 1km:manuscript in file	Photo numbers [D] ABCDE L61/1-49
DOCUMENTS & COLLECT-IONS	L Class Author : date : title : journal or publisher : volume : note Specimens or collections	
[C]	H1 description : :site record:OS (Arch Division): :ST 49SE14	

24.

Fig. 3 Example of MDS record media: Locality.

ARCHAEOLOGY

Card of		

					Institution : identity number		Part
File					KIRMG:1976.60		

IDENTIFICATION C

Simple name	D	Materials keyword/detail		Number
blade		bronze	System	D

Full name or classified identification
Childe,V.G.:1931 D Identifier : date D

DATING C

Object period or date
(Late) Bronze Age

Dating method Cross reference Researcher : date D

COLLECTION OR EXCAVATION C

Site name	Site number			Lat Long	Value & units/accuracy	
Oriel Road				NGR	NT 2721 9164	D

Place name/detail
Oriel Road & Kirkcaldy & Kirkcaldy Parish & Fife

Context		Context period or date	
Cist 1			D

Locality detail

Collection method	Collector or excavator : date	Find number	
excavated	Childe,V.G.:1931		D

ACQUISITION C

Acquisition method Acquired from : date
gift anon:(pre) 1973

	D Price		Conditions Yes/No	D	Valuation : date	D

DESCRIPTION C

Condition keyword/detail Completeness keyword/detail
fair incomplete (approx. 10% missing)

STORE

Store : date	Recorder : date
J12	Glaister,J.M.:1979

1/12/75

84

DESCRIPTION

Dimension measured	value & units/accuracy	Dimension measured	value & units/accuracy
length	4 cms		
width	1.2 × 4 cms		

Inscription	Method	Position		D
Mark				
Transcription	Detail			D
Description				

Part : aspect : description keyword/detail

blade:manufacture:hammered (from rod)

C

PROCESS

Conservation	Other process	Method/detail : operator : date : detail	Cross reference	D
Reproduction				
Conservation				
Reproduction				

stabilised:NMAS:(pre) 1973

C

DOCUMENTATION

L	Class	Author : date : title : journal or publisher : volume : detail	Drawing or photo
H	described	Reedie,K.:1972:Neolithic and Bronze Age Culture in Fife:Edin. Univ. Dept. Prehist. Arch.	
H		Childe,V.G.:1943-4: :PSAS:LXXVIII:p. 109	
		:1958:Invent. Arch.: :G.B. 32	

C

NOTES

index headings:death customs & materials & class

C

Fig. 4 Example of MDS record media: Archaeological Object.

85

Computerisation of excavation records and archaeological archives has already been carried out for museum based excavating units, for example, the Department of Urban Archaeology, Museum of London. Such projects can provide cross-referencing indexes and simple statistics as an aid to writing up the final reports. These facilities can be used by any excavating unit, whether attached to a museum of not.

A new facility, the Sample Computerisation Project, can also be used by any institution with collections, such as units. This project can be used to test the internal consistency of manual records, and their compatibility for future data-base work (Stewart, 1982).

In addition to advisory and computerisation facilities, the MDA's own record media (Figure 3) can be purchased by non-museum institutions. Figure 4 illustrates the MDS Archaeology Object card;

Addendum

The MDA has also recently published a guide to the use of micro-computers in British museums which is the first review of current software and micro-computer equipment (Light and Roberts, 1984).

Summary

Mention has been made of museums' role as centres of information, housing as they do, both physical items and their asociated documentation. A documentation system, (whether computerised or not) to cover both theoretical and pratical aspects is implicit in this new role. Investigation of data-bases and bridging mechanisms may assist in the 'recycling' of archaeological data, not only for those in the field but for curatorial and other users of these centres of information.

I should like to stress how much the MDA would like to work with other organisations which represent British archaeology to provide a comprehensive system for archaeological documentation; to pool experience that the MDA has gained in cataloguing collections for museums, which after all are organisations which store, conserve and display archaeological collections, in perpetuity.

In conclusion to any discussion about future 'information systems' in archaeology one could fittingly rephrase what Mr Kenneth Eaker, Minister of State for Industry and Information Technology said at the launch of IT82 (Aslib Information, 1982):-

'. . . we are entering an exciting era, we are seeing the museum of the future and the excavation of the future emerge from the realms of science fiction and become a reality.

This is happening through the application of microelectronics to the control of machines, to computing, to documentation.

An enormous range of these activities is being transformed by Information Technology – we are indeed a lucky generation to see the first fruits of this revolution.'

References

Aslib information, 1982 *Information Technology year is upon us.* Aslib information, 20(1), 1982, 4.
Atkinson, M.F. 1979 Database systems. *Journal of Documentation,* 35, 1979, 49–91.
Atkinson, R. J. C. 1955 A national index of archaeological collections. *Museums Journal,* 54(10), 1955, 255–259.
A.M.B. 1978 Ancient Monuments Board for England. Committee for Rescue Archaeology. *Scientific treatment of material from rescue archaeology. A report by a Working Party of the Committee for Rescue Archaeology of the Ancient Monuments Board for England.* London: HMSO (for the Directorate of Ancient Monuments and Historical Buildings.)
Bezeczky, T. 1981 *Draft of the Hungarian archaeological data base.* (Vezprem, Hungary, September 1981.) unpublished typescript.
B. L. R. & D. Dept, 1977 The British Library Research and Development Department. *Problems of Information handling in Archaeology. Report of a seminar.* British Library, Reasearch and Development Report. No. 5329 London: British Library (for the Research and Development Dept).
Clarke, David L. 1978 *Analytical Archaeology* (second edition, revised) London: Methuen and Co. Ltd.
Cooper, J. A. 1981 The National Scheme for Geological Site Documentation. Annual Report, 1980. *The Geological Curator,* 3 (2/3), 1981, 153–157.
CBA 1978 Council for British Archaeology *Computer retrieval of archaeological information. CBA Day School 28th September 1978.* London: CBA.
Cowgill, George L. 1967, Computer applications in archaeology. *Computers and the Humanities,* 2 (1), 1967, 17–23.
Date, C. J. 1977 *An introduction to database systems.* (second edition). The Systems Programming Series. Reading, Massachusetts: Addison-Wesley Publishing Company.
Fagg, A. 1981. Information Technology: what is it? *CCTA News,* 8, 1981, 3.
Flood, Steven, 1982. Review of Orna and Pettit *"Information handling in museums". Journal of Information Science,* 3 (6), 1982, 295–296.
Flood, S. W. and Perring, F. H. (compilers) 1978 *A handbook for local biological records centres.* Biology Curators Group and Biological Records Centre.
Gaines, S. and Gaines, W. 1980. Future trends in computer applications. *American Antiquity,* 45(3), 1980, 462–471.
Graham, Ian 1981. *Micro-computers for archaeological excavation recording. Intelligent computer terminals for archaeological site recording.* Report to the British Library on project Number SI/G/216. Final Report. London: Institute of Archaeology.
G. B. 1981a Great Britain, Department of Industry. *Information Technology Year* 1982 London: D. I.
G. B. 1981b Great Britain, Department of Industry. Information Technology Division. *Information technology. The use of electronic information.* London: D. I.
Hancock, E. G. 1980. One of those dreadful combats – a surviving display from William Bullock's London Museum, 1807–1818. *Museum Journal,* 79(4), 1980, 172–175.

Higgins, S. C. 1981. Government policy towards information technology (IT). CCTA News, 7, 1981, 3–4.

Inform, 1982 Information Technology Year 1982. *Inform*, 42, 1982, 1.

Lagrande, M. S. 1978. A comparative study of the logical structure of information recorded about material objects in computerized data bases in archaeology, history of art and related fields. In Barocchi, P. and Bisogni, F. 1978, *International Conference on Automatic Processing of Art History Data and Documents*. Pisa: Scuola Normale Superiore.

Lane, J. E. 1981. *Microprocessors and information handling*. Manchester: NCC.

Le Maitre, Jacques 1978. *La rationalisation des systemes de traitement de l'information documentaire en archeologie*. Publications du Centre de Recherches Archeologiques. Paris: Editions du Centre National de la Recherche Scientifique.

Light. R. B. 1982. Today's microcomputers for museum documentation? *Museums Journal*, 1982, 82(2), 77–8.

Light, R. B. and Roberts, D. A. 1982. International museum data standards and experiments in data transfer. *MDA Occasional Paper* 5. Duxford, Cambridgeshire: M.D.A.

Light, R.B. and Roberts, D.A. 1984. Microcomputers in museums. *MDA Occasional Paper* 7. Duxford, Cambridgeshire: M.D.A.

Michelmore, D. J. H. 1981. The Storage of archaeological records. In Partington-Omar, A. and White, A. J. (ed) 1981 *Archaeological storage*. Society of Museum Archaeologists and Yorkshire & Humberside Federation of Museums and Art Galleries. pp. 25–26.

Moffat, J. and Webb, E. 1982. Database Management Systems and Radiocarbon Dating. *Computer Applications in Archaeology*, 1981, 76–78.

Museum 1978. Museums and computers. *Museum*, XXX, 3/4 1978 (whole issue).

MDA 1979 Museum Documentation Association. MDA Museum Codes. *MDA Occasional Paper* 2. Duxford, Cambridgeshire: MDA.

MDA 1980. Museum Documentation Association. *Archaeology Object card instructions*. Museum Documentation System. Duxford, Cambridgeshire: MDA.

MDA 1982. Museum Documentation Association. *Guide to the Museum Documentation System*. Second Edition. Duxford, Cambridgeshire: MDA.

Museum of London, Department of Urban Archaeology 1980 *Site Manual. Part 1: The written record*. London: Museum of London.

Nora, S. and Minc,, A. 1980. *The computerisation of society. A report to the President of France*. London: MIT Press.

Oikawa, A. 1981. A jomon Kaizuka database in Japan. In Vezina, R. 1981. *Computerised Inventory standards for works of art*. Conference proceedings. Montreal, Quebec: La Corporationdes Editions Fides. pp. 78–80.

Piggott, Stuart 1976. *Ruins in a Landscape. Essays in antiquarianism*. Edinburgh: Edinburgh University Press.

Rhodes, M. 1980. Some thoughts concerning the definition of the aims and objectives in the development of excavation archives. *Museum Archaeologist*, 5, 1980, 28–35.

Roberts, D. Andrew 1982. CIDOC Technical Standards Working Group. *MDA Information*, 5(9), 1982, 46.

RCHM 1978. Royal Commission on Historic Monuments (England). *Survey of surveys, 1978. A review of local archaeological field survey and recording*. London: OHMS.

Scholtz, Sandra and Chenhall, Robert, G. 1976. Archaeological data banks in theory and practice. *American Antiquity*, 41(2), 1976, 89–96

Schollar, Irwin, 1982. Thrity years of computer archaeology and the future, or looking backwards and forwards at the same time while trying not to twist one's neck. *Computer Applications in Archaeology*, 1982, 189–198.

Sharpe, T. and Howe. S.R. 1982, Family expeditions – the museum outdoors. *Museums Journal*, 1982 82(3), 143–7.

Stewart, Jennifer D. 1980a. Integrated excavation and museum recording systems: methods, theories and problems. *Museum Archaeologist*, 5, 1980, 11–27.

Stewart, Jennifer D. 1980b. Environmental Record Centres – a decade of progress? *MDA Occasional Paper* 3. Duxford, Cambridge: MDA.

Stewart, Jennifer D. 1980c. A summary of local environmental record centres in Britain. *Museums Journal*, 80(3), 1980, 161–164.

Stewart, Jennifer D. (ed.) 1980d. Microcomputers in Archaeology. Proceedings of a seminar held in the Institute of Archaeology, 18 June 1980, with related articles. *MDA Occasional Paper* 4. Duxford, Cambridge: MDA.

Stewart, Jennifer, D. 1982. Computerising archaeological records – a progress report on the work of the MDA. *Computer Applications in Archaeology*, 1982, 4–10.

Stewart, Jennifer D. (in press). MDA, MDS and computerised archaeology. *Computer Applications in Archaeology*, 1981 (in press)

Technology and Conservation 1978. A well regulated environment . . . saving collections and costs. *Technology and Conservation*, 2, 1978, 5–7.

Technology and Conservation 1979. Computerized checks and balances..for fuel/Labor savings in museums. *Technology and Conservation*, 3, 1979, 5–9.

Technology and Conservation 1980. Energy survey: report on conservation programs and problems. *Technology and Conservation*, 2, 1980, 28–30.

Whallon, Robert 1972. The computer in archaeology: a critical survey. *Computers and the Humanitites*, 7(1), 1972, 29–45.

Wilcock, J. D. 1973. A general survey of computer applications in archaeology. *Science and Archaeology*, 9, 1973, 17–21.

Whittlin, Alma S. 1970. *Museums: in search of a usable future*. Cambridge, Massachusetts: MIT Press.

CHAPTER 8

ONLINE INFORMATION RETRIEVAL, DATA-BASES AND NETWORKS

Charles Oppenheim

Derwent Publications Ltd.

Online information retrieval means the user interrogating a remote computer – and by remote, I mean anything from a few yards away to literally thousands of miles away – using a terminal and employing some telecommunications link. The user is in direct contact with the computer – that is what the word 'online' means. Input into the computer, and output from the computer is fast, so the search takes little time. Online computer systems are nearly always time-shared, that is to say several users can access the same computer at the same time. However, because the computer responds so fast, the user gets the impression that he or she is in sole contact with the computer.

There are three main strands in the history of online information retrieval. For many years, publishers have printed books and journals, but in recent years they have gone over to computer typesetting. This involves a computer holding the information in machine-readable form, including the printing instructions (upper case here, bold characters there, indent here, italicise that, etc.).

So, the first strand to our history is the trend towards computer typesetting. The second strand is the vast increase in the power of computers over the past 20 years. This means a computer can store more information more economically and process it faster than ever before.

The third strand, and the one which really turned out to be the trigger for the explosive growth in online shown in the last ten years, has been the vast improvement in telecommunications netweorks. As a result, data can be transferred reliably, cheaply and qickly from one location to another.

The advent of online information retrieval is therefore due to the convergence of three sorts of new technology – typesetting, computers and telecommunications. The first experimental commercial online services started in the USA at the start of the 1970's. The entrepeneurs were System Development Corportation (SDC), followed soon after by Lockheed Aircraft. These two are still the dominant names in the business. Lockheed's turnover is about $10,000,000 p.a., and SDC's is about $5,000,000 p.a.

The basic technology

All a user requires is three things: a terminal, a telephone and a modem. 'Modem' is the shorthand name for a modulator/demodulator.

You also need to get passwords which entitle you to access the computers and the telecommunication networks involved in online information retrieval. The bureaucracy involved in this is minimal.

The terminal can be any standard type of terminal incorporating a visual display unit and/or a printer so that you can see what you are sending to the remote computer, and how it is responding. The terminal might be devoted solely to online use, or you might use it for other purposes, such as accessing a Computer Centre, as a microcomputer or as a word processor, perhaps.

The telephone should, ideally, give you a direct outside line. The noise which is transmitted between your terminal and the remote computer is a high pitched whistle, and a switchboard operator may cut you off if she hears it and thinks you've got a 'number unobtainable' tone.

In order to convert this high pitched whistle into the alphanumeric characters recognised by your terminal, you need a modem. You can hire a modem from British Telecom which is incorporated into the telephone handset. Alternatively, you can purchase an acoustic coupler; this is not quite as good as a modem in the telephone handset because you get more telecommunications noise on the line, but it is portable and so not tied to one particular telephone.

Most online information retrieval operations are conducted at either 30 characters per second, or increasingly, at 120 characters per second. You will often hear people refer to 'baud' instead of characters per second. Very roughly, one character per second is ten baud, so 300 baud means thirty characters per second.

I now want to look at the telecommunications links involved in online information retrieval. Of course, your terminal could be wired directly to the remote computer. This is likely if the computer is in your own establishement or if you obtain a leased line to a remote computer. Leased lines are only cost effective for frequent use of the remote computer.

The second, and more usual method, is to use a public network. You can telephone the remote computer directly, or you might telephone a local node and get switched through to the remote computer. Incidentally, the term 'remote computer' is not the normal term used in this business; it is more normal to call the computer the 'host computer' and to call the commercial organisation that mounts the host computer either the 'host computer service', 'the spinner', or sometimes even just 'the vendor'. There are many host computer services in operation throughout the world, but the ones you are most likely to come across the Lockheed DIALOG (their computer is based in California); SDC ORBIT, part of Burroughs Computers, and with host computers in California and Japan; the European Space Agency's Information Retrieval Service (sometimes also known as Dialtech) – their computer is in Italy; Pergamon-Infoline, part of the Pergamon empire with a London based computer; and Derwent/SDC, a joint venture between Derwent Publications and SDC, whose computer is in Woking. There are many other hosts, scattered all over the world.

Data-bases and Data-banks

It is my intention to keep the amount of jargon in this paper to a minimum, but there are one or two other terms that need to be defined. These are data-bases and data-banks.

A data-base, sometimes also called a 'file', is, from the point of view of online information retrieval, an abstracting or indexing service in machine-readable form. These are services which do not answer a particular question – such as what were the exports of tin from Bolivia in 1981? – but tell you the details of some original document in which the answer to your question can be found. A brief abstract, or summary, of the document may well also be supplied. In other words, a data-base supplies you with one or more references, which you then have to get hold of from your own library or from some other library. These data-bases are produced by the so-called data-base producers. Data-base producers can be organisations in the data-base production business to make money, can be learned societies, government departments, research associations, and so on. A given data-base may be available on just one host computer service, or on many.

In contrast to data-bases, on online data-bank actually provdes hard data. This data might be numeric, such as the boiling point of water, or could be textual, like a name and address. Numeric data-banks are often mounted on specialist hosts who provide the software required to manipulate the data, e.g. make forecasts, correlations and statistical overviews. Once again, all sorts of organisations produce data-banks, governments being particularly prolific. An online data-bank may be on just one host, or on many.

Another jargon term worth noting is PTT – the shorthand for the organisations that hold the monopoly rights to telecommunications networks. In the USA, such networks are not run by Governmental bodies, but by private enterprise, and names you are likely to come across are Telenet and Tymnet. In the UK, you are likely to hear about IPSS (International Packet Switchstream) and PSS (Packet Switchstream), both run by British Telecom, and in Europe you will hear about Euronet DIANE, run by the consortium of European PTT's. There are plans to integrate all these various networks into one network covering the entire earth.

To summarise, online information retrieval involves four parties – the searcher, the telecommunications network, the host computer service and the data-base/data-bank producer. Sometimes the data-base producer is the same organisation as the host computer service, but this isn't common. The searcher, using simple dial up procedures, accesses the host computer, selects the data-base or data-bank of choice, and carries out the search before logging off.

Costs of Online Searching

The costs of online can be split into two parts. There are the initial capital costs to get the necessary equipment. Then there are the costs incurred when you actually run an online search.

The initial capital costs for a terminal and a modem can be a couple of thousand pounds. However, it is likely that some, or all of the necessary equipment is already available.

Most host computer services do not charge for a password although some do. There are nominal annual fees to maintain passwords to some of the telecommunications networks. So you can see that, apart from the hardware, the amount of 'up front' payments you have to make are minimal.

What about the costs of doing the searches? The most common arrangement is a low or zero cost for a password and you are then charged for every online search you do. In some cases there is an annual 'up front' sum to pay, and then each online search is free, or very low cost – but only a minority of systems work that way.

The online search costs comprise in most cases a series of components as follows:

cost per hour to connect to the chosen data-base/data-bank (this cost includes a cut for the host computer service);
telecommunications charges (usually based partly on time spent online, partly on the amount of data which has travelled to and fro);
costs of any online types – if these are charged for cost of any offline prints ordered, (plus, of course, searcher's time, depreciation of equipment, etc.).

Typical data-base connect hour charges would be £15 – £50 per hour, typical offline print charges are 5p to 25p per print. Overall, a typical online search can be said to cost about £1 per minute plus the cost of online and offline prints run off. This figure includes telecommunications costs, but not searcher's time.

Advantages of online information retrieval

There are two types of advantage of online information retrieval over the traditional methods of information retrieval used up till now – in other words over searching through printed volumes of text. There are the tangible advantages, immediately recognised, and the intangible advantages.

93

Let us look at the tangible advantages first:

1. You have access to many data-bases and data-banks – far more than any library or any organisation could hope to subscribe to.
2. Some of the data-bases and data-banks available online indeed have no printed equivalent, so the only way to get access to them is by online.
3. A printed service you can normally search two ways – by author or by subject. With online systems you can search by these two ways, but also by many other parameters, such as by publication date, place where the author works, words in the title, by subject matter classification, and so on – and you can combine these parameters at will: for example, a search for all papers on microprocessors emanating from Leeds University, virtually impossible using a printed source, is extremely easy online.
4. A very important advantage is your ability to amend the search strategy in the light of the output. If you get too many hits, you refine the strategy down; too few hits and you broaden the strategy; because of the nearly instantanous response, this still means fast searches.
5. If you order offline prints, they look extremely professional – good enough to hand to the person asking for the search without any retyping, editing, etc.
6. Searchers are quick and relatively cheap.
7. The searches are up to date – online data-bases get updated very quickly.
8. Online systems can handle very large files containing literally millions of records with ease.
9. You only pay for the searches you do. Thus, if you search a given source only once a year, you don't have the expense of having to subscribe to it.
10. Online offers several spin-off features of value, such as online SDI (selective dissemination of information), in which your subject interest is checked against each update of the files, and you are automatically sent items of potential interest; online document ordering where by a simple command you order photocopies of items you have identified as relevant; and crossfile searching, allowing you to run a complex search against one data-base after another with minimum typing in.

What about the intangible advantages? There is less clerical effort involved – no longer do you have laboriously to transcribe the information you have found, as you get a printout instead. Also, for the vast majority of people, online information retrieval is FUN – people far prefer it to arduously wading through printed subject indexes, and abstracts. However, as with all things in life, there is another side to the coin. There are certain caveats about online.

Firstly, in general only recent material is available online. This is for the simple reason that only recently has textual material been phototypeset. So, if you want to search back in time, you will still have a lot of printed works to go through.

Secondly, not all subject areas are well covered by online information retrieval services. Perhaps the outstanding example of such a poorly served area is archaeology! I am not aware of any other learned subject so poorly treated, although history comes a close second.

Thirdly, for small organisations, the initial equipment costs are high – although, as I have indicated, online offers overall cost advantages over manual searching.

Fourthly, there is Sod's (or Murphy's) Law of Online Information Retrieval. This states that the chances of telecommunications failure/system crashes/other disasters are directly proportional to the number of people wishing to see the search, and their importance.

Fifthly, there are too many systems around and too little standardisation between them – so there is too much for the searcher to learn.

Finally, there are too few data-banks actually answering the question, as opposed to data-bases telling you where you can find the answer to your question.

I want to now look at the structure of online data-bases, the techniques for searching them, and the data-bases of interest to archaeologists.

The structure of a database

Each online data-base comprises a series, maybe several millions, of records, each of which has a series of alphanumeric characters – such as author's name, details of the source document, subject index words, classification marks, and so on. These subdivisions are known as 'fields'.

A computer has two ways of handling a set of records. The first way, the so-called linear (or serial) file way, lists an accession number, and against that accession number the entire record is held; it then goes on to the next accession number, the next accession number and so on. The other way is to use an inverted file. In this case, against any given mark (e.g. an author's name, a classification symbol) is listed all the accession numbers that have such a record.

When on online search is run, asking for example. 'How many items are there with the word 'Bolivia' in the title?', the computer checks the inverted file and notes the accession numbers of those items answering the query and reports back to the searcher how many items it has found. If you then ask 'How many of those items also have the author's name 'Jones' present?', the computer compares lists of accession numbers for the two queries and reports how many have the same accession number present. If you then ask to see the hits printed out, the computer switches to the serial file, identifies the required accession numbers, and prints out the details of those items.

The field or fields to be searched can be specified; each data-base will have a default option, which it will search if you don't specify a field. This default option is often called the 'basic index'.

Boolean logic

The most common way of searching an online system is using Boolean logic. The major Boolean logic terms are AND, OR, NOT. I have just described an example of an AND search – those items with Bolivia and Jones present. The next sort of search, using OR logic, would be, for example 'All records containing the works MICROPROCESSOR OR CHIP'. The final sort of Boolean seach logic is NOT logic. For example, you want all records containing the word Telecommunications, but NOT the word Plessey. In the case of AND and OR logic, it does not matter in what order the search is specified – thus 'Bolivia AND Jones' is the same as 'Jones AND Bolivia'; 'Microprocessor OR chip' is the same as 'Chip OR microprocessor'. But you will appreciate that 'Telecommunications NOT Plessey' will give a totally different set of hits from 'Plessey NOT Telecommunications'.

In all Boolean logic searching, the computer searches the inverted file checking for accession numbers in common – a trivially easy task for a computer, so Boolean logic searches are very fast. However, you can get misleading answers – the so-called false drops. For example, imagine you are interested in the use of sodium catalysts to manufacture lead. If you enter Sodium AND catalysts AND manufacture AND lead, you may pick up a record on the use of lead catalysts in the manufacture of sodium. So, although Boolean logic is logical(!) and rapid, it is not always perfect.

One way around the problems of Boolean logic is to use word adjacency searching, or string searching, which is employed by most hosts. In this case you ask that certain terms appear next to each other, e.g. BALANCE OF PAYMENTS, or SODIUM CATALYST. Such a search has to be carried out through the serial file, and can take longer than a Boolean logic search – but it ensures fewer false drops.

The data-bases of interest to archaeology

The first thing to note is that a number of the well known indexing and asbstrating services in archaeology, for example *Art and Archeology Technical Abstracts, British Archaeological Abstracts* and *Nordic Archaeological Abstracts,* are not available online.

There are a number of large data-bases which happen to cover archaeology amongst other topics – for example NTIS, the US Government Reports data-base, and two geological data-bases, GeoRef and GeoArchive. However, all of these pale into insignificance when compared with the French data-base on the humanities produced by the CDSH (Centre de Documentation Sciences Humaines). CDSH has developed a major data-base called FRANCIS, comprising some 600,000 records, most of them with keywords and abstracts and growing by some 75,000 items a year, taken from some 8,000 source publications. The data-base covers all human sciences, such as philosophy, education, sociology, linguistics, and archaeology. There are printed phototypeset abstracting journals produced by CDSH on archaeology, and you can lease tapes of the archaeology material from CDSH for in-house searching on your own computer: to cover all of art, archaeology and prehistory from the period 1972 to 1980 (the dates refer to publication dates of the source items) would cost you 63,500 French Francs in leasing of tapes charges. As an alternative, you can search the FRANCIS data-base online.

FRANCIS is available on two hosts. It is available in full on Telesystemes Questel – known as FRANCIS. A portion of the data-base is loaded on ESA-IRS and is known as PASCAL. The number of archaeologial references in the full FRANCIS data-base in the fields of prehistory, art and archaeology are about 100,000 – 140,000 in the period 1972 to date, growing by some 20,000 items a year. Most of the material was originally in the French or English languages and the majority were periodical articles.

As far as I can tell, there are no data-banks of archaeological interest available on any of the major hosts throughout the world.

Future developments in online services

What of the future? What developments are likely in online information retrieval services in the next few years? Here are some thoughts:

1. There will be a trend towards data-banks rather than data-bases.
2. The entering of chemical structures, and their output onto screens will be much improved in the next few years.
3. More data-base indexes will be offered – these advise the searcher which are the best data-bases or data-banks to search for a particular concept.
4. There will be moves towards greater standardisation, both in the command languages employed by the various host computer services and the ways each record is split into fields and how these fields are handled.
5. I also forsee a shakeout in the online market – there are too many host services chasing too little business at the moment.

There will also be dramatic changes in telecommunications. We will soon have high speed, noise-free high bandwidth systems – especially satellite based systems – coming available. These will facilitate efficient and fast transmission of data, and at long last it will be possible to transmit graphic material – tables, graphs, drawings – from the computer to the terminal. These high speed networks will interconnect with local networks, so that anyone will have access to the system.

The area of display of graphic data is a particularly interesting one. It is frustrating for a searcher, when he or she gets output from an online search, to find the text referring to graphic material ('chemical compounds of formula I, where R can be hydrogen or chlorine'), but being unable to see what this graphic material is. The graphic material could be sent down the telecommunications networks, but bandwidth limitations of the present systems preclude this. Also, graphic material takes up a lot of computer storage.

There are other possibilities to consider, though. The searcher could use an intelligent terminal, which would store the accession numbers of the hits. The terminal could then switch to a local store of graphics data, perhaps on microfilm or on videodisc, and call up each accession number in turn.

Intelligent terminals will be used increasingly by searchers in years to come. They will do such jobs as translating one search software to another, for storing, editing, sorting merging and printing output from searches (this has copyright implications, of course), and they can be used for remembering the various protocols for accessing the numerous hosts. They could also be used for creating mini-data-bases for in-house use taken from online searches. The searcher might add his or her own additional indexing too. These changes will make online searching cheaper and easier.

Online information retrieval is a very well established feature in science and technology and business. I forsee a massive increase in its use in other areas, such as the humanities, in which it has had not much penetration thus far. There is a painless way to ensure that archaeology gets well covered. The only difference between data-bases and data-banks of archaeological relevance and the online services that I have been discussing is that they are only available to closed groups, whereas online systems are available to anyone. It would be logical to make your data-bases and data-banks available on the major hosts. You would recoup some of your development costs, for of course the data-base/data-bank producer gets royalties every time his data-base or data-bank is searched. You would also be making the wealth of archaeological information you have ammassed more readily available. I strongly recommend that you consider entering this market.

CHAPTER 9

BIBLIOGRAPHICAL DATA-BASES IN ARCHAEOLOGY

KRAS: KEYWORDED REFERENCES TO ARCHAEOLOGICAL SCIENCE

Roger Martlew

Department of Archaeology, Leicester University

Bibliographical information in archaeology.

The project to set up a data-base of references to archaeological science at Leicester University is organised by Dr Myra Shackley, and has received financial support in the form of grants from the Manpower Services Commission. The aim of the project is to establish and operate an online bibliographical information service for archaeological science, the first of its kind. References with a publication date later than 1975 have been collected, covering as wide a geographical range as possible; sources are mainly British, Western European and American, but reports from countries further afield such as Eastern Europe, Russia, China and Japan are included.

The need for such a reference source has been expressed several times over the past decade. In 1976 the CBA and the British Library organised a seminar on "The problems of Information Handling in Archaeology" (British Library Board, 1977). Contributors from a wide variety of backgrounds expressed their feelings on the kind of information service which they would like to see in archaeology, mainly in connection with the existing services offered by the CBA's *Bibliography* and *British Archaeological Abstracts*. The commonest demand was for a means of scanning the available literature not in a specialist's own field, but in other areas which may not be directly relevant to a limited field of research. The purposes of this scanning reflect the very different demands which are made upon a centralised information service: "general awareness" information is required so that individuals can keep in touch with developments throughout the discipline, as against searches for information on highly specialised topics.

A second need identified at the CBA/BL seminar was for adequate coverage of foreign journals: most contributors appeared to be satisfied with European and American references, but others would like to be guided to reports from countries such as Russia and Japan.

Further comments emphasised the division into "general" and "specific" information outlined above. A data-base covering a limited subject may be searched on a general level not only by non-specialists in the subject, but also by people from outside the discipline altogether. Those who do not have ready access to the resources of an academic library would find the information very difficult, time-consuming, and expensive to locate, and are likely to miss associated topics in other subjects areas.

The proposals which have been made for filling this gap in resources have not been taken up on any scale (Amis, 1970; Celoria, 1971). The suggestion that individuals should spend a day in their nearest library once a month, searching the literature on the off-chance of finding something relevant, is not practical. Archaeological references are scattered throughout a number of primary and secondary sources, abstracting and indexing services (Hasso, 1978, 23–32), and are often widely scattered on a library's shelves. A similarly dispersed array of online services (ibid., 32–40) contains small percentages of references often covering only limited periods. With figures such as 18 entries between 1974 and 1976, out of a total of 21,000 records on one data-base, it is hardly surprising that several of these services seem to have lost interest in archaeology (ibid., 32). The organisation of volunteers to contribute abstracts or book-lists to existing journals is severely limited by the rising costs of traditional printing and publishing, and would require considerable motivation to be sustained indefinitely.

Some abstracting services already cover scientific material in archaeology, but only in limited ways: the C.B.A.'s *British Archaeological Abstracts* only concerns itself with material of major importance, and *Art and Archaeeology Technical Abstracts* is orientated towards museum and conservation work. Any developments towards an efficient information service in archaeological science must avoid duplication of effort, but the poor coverage by centralised secondary sources has already allowed this to happen. Many specialists and academics have built up their own card-indexes over the years, and may have reservations about making them freely available in view of the considerable amount of time and effort invested in them. Current developments in technology demand a reconsideration of the tenurial rights to information, as the possibility of rapid and cheap information flow between large computerised stores becomes not only a reality, but a commercially exploited fact.

Of more immediate concern, however, is the efficiency of the traditional methods of handling bibliographical information. Apart from the multiplication of effort throughout the country, there is a tendency for individual card-indexes to be idiosyncratic, containing an identical core of important and easily accessible material, but falling off rapidly in quality with references on the fringes of an individual's research area. Academics and specialists have little time for prolonged searches through partially relevant material, in the hope of adding to their bibliography by serendipity. Existing abstracting services in archaeology have been criticised for poor coverage (Miller, 1974, 29), and the dispersed and small-scale nature of many archaeological reference collections has added to the problems (Hasso, 1978, 188–93).

Although the British Museum Research Laboratory and *Art and Archaeology Technical Abstracts* are involved in the computerisation of bibliographical resources, the full potential of computers has been sadly neglected in the wider field of archaeological bibliographies. Nothing has come of the proposal of the 1976 seminar on "The Problems of Information Handling in Archaeology", that the C.B.A. should institute a pilot project for the computerisation of its abstracting services (British Library Board, 1977). Unlike the wide variety of information from excavations, bibliographical data are well-defined and have been computerised by libraries and other disciplines for some time. Familiarity with information systems using this type of data may encourage the development of the more complex information services which would be necessary for archaeology as a whole.

The establishment of the KRAS data-base at Leicester

The initial one-year project has established a data-base of about 2000 references on archaeological science, covering the 7-year period from 1976 to 1982. This compares with the 8,000 general archaeological references in *British Archaeological Abstracts,* covering 14 years from 1968. The process of keywording takes less time than compiling abstracts, but obviously provides less information on each reference.

Decisions on which references to include and which to omit have in many cases been forced by the limited time available at this stage, although the pressure to produce an operational system in one year has had some beneficial effects. The collection and typing in of references is a tedious operation – a mammoth French undertaking to computerise the holdings on archaeology of several libraries collapsed through boredom and lack of motivation (Le Maitre et al., 1980); a similar project at Harvard also ground to a halt in the face of the enormity of the task (McPherron, A, pers. comm.).

One decision forced by the lack of time was to avoid listing separately the specialist reports which appear in excavation monographs, or as appendices to reports in journals. Very often these are not detailed in contents tables, and their inclusion as separate entries in the data-base, as more than just a title and general keyword, would produce an overwhelming amount of information in the form of lists of the species, minerals, bones, etc. with which the reports deal individually. Details on this scale require a data-base project of their own, and there is no reason why this important information should not be made available alongside the more general bibliographical data in the future.

The shortage of time for the establishment of the data-base also meant that the information retrieval packages which were already available on the Leicester computer had to be used. INFOL-2 was the only package which could be used at Leicester when the project commenced, but RIQS (Remote Information Query Sustem) was implemented shortly afterwards. Both of these packages leave a lot to be desired: RIQS is very greedy of computer memory and INFOL has a complicated command language which is not, to use the jargon, "user friendly"; neither packages (as implemented at Leicester) can deal easily with lower-case letters, so that all print-outs are in block capitals. However, the University mainframe is scheduled for replacement in 1984, and negotitiations are already under way for the acquisition of much more powerful data-base software.

Retrieval of information from KRAS can be by any bibliographical detail – author, consecutive words in a title, journal, etc., or by combinations of keywords. Some journals (such as the *Journal of Archaeological Science* and *Archaeometry)* already ask authors to include keywords with the abstracts of their papers, but there seems to be little attempt to preserve consistency within the words chosen. This is of vital importance when keywords are to be used in a computerised retrieval system, and it is usual to compile a thesaurus of acceptable terms, with indications of preferred synonyms and alternatives. Computers are remorselessly literal, and unless the difference between "archaeology" and "archeology" has been allowed for by the programmer, the computer will treat them as totally different words. Some systems have 'dictionary' or equivalence files which allow synonyms or thousands of spellings to be checked, but neither of the current retrieval packages at Leicester has this facility. Terms which are exactly or even loosely synonymous must be represented by only one keyword for maximum efficiency: spectroscopy, spectrography and spectrometry seem to be used synonymously by different authors, but only the first has been adopted as a keyword to prevent all three having to be typed in for a search; the context should make intentional differences in meaning clear. "Stone" and "rock" both appeared in the keyword list of a recent paper (Kempe, 1982), and although it is relatively easy to tell the computer to look for *both* "stone" *and* "rock", it should not be up to the person using the system to have to enter lists of synonyms, or consider every possible alternative term for each enquiry.

The KRAS keywords endeavour to follow the pattern of general subject, specific and associated subjects, geographical region, period. The order of these items is irrelevant to the computer, but inclusion or non-inclusion can be very significant for the user. Authors tend to supply keywords on the basis of what is contained in their article without attempting to show limits of relevance. General terms such as "Europe" and "Neolithic" may be thought sufficient, when in fact the paper concentrates on two or three countries during a more limited period. A list of the countries and an indication of the date range would prevent the reference being retrieved by someone interested only in the whole of Europe during the whole of the Neolithic. Imprecise terms are often deliberately used when interpretations differ between specialists, or are being challenged by current research. Inevitably the greatest problems are with chronology, but it will be a useful side-effect if the application of information technology produces a clarification of terms and ideas in archaeology.

Keywords are not intended to be as comprehensive as an index, and the compromise inevitably results in a certain amount of redundant information – known as 'false drops' in the jargon – being retrieved. As the size of the data-base increases, more sophisticated search strategies and facilities are necessary to keep this to an acceptable minimum. A reference list or thesaurus for use by authors would be one way of increasing consistency of keywording in the various journals which use the system at present; other journals should definitely be encouraged to adopt keywords, with or without abstracts. If journals listed their keywords under the headings of general and detailed subject, region and period, it would help authors think logically about the words they are choosing.

The KRAS information service

Subscribers to KRAS will receive an index of keywords, authors and journals on microfiche, so that they can get a good idea of subject coverage, check spelling and usage, and define keyword combinations before submitting a request. This is the only practical way to distribute the information at low cost; a supplementary charge on large amounts of printed output means that the cost of one fiche, about 16p, compares with a cost for hard-copy of about £15.

Requests for information from the KRAS data-base will usually be made on pre-printed forms, but programs have been written to allow users to access the data-base directly from their own computer terminal or microcomputer, using a modem to link the terminal to the telephone system; university-based subscribers are able to use the rapidly expanding universities' computer network. By the end of the decade, if not sooner, it will be possible to sit at a terminal in one university and directly control a job being executed on the computer of any other university in the country. Communication between computers in, for example, county Units will also be more efficient, but may be more expensive if reliant on commercially controlled networks.

The cost of an online enquiry to the KRAS data-base will obviously depend on the cost of the telephone call. Output can be directed to a lineprinter at Leicester to be returned by post, or listings of a few references at the terminal can be accommodated within a phone call of only a few minutes. Taking advantage of off-peak rates and cheap routes, 30 references can be obtained within about five minutes at a cost of only 65p. Full bibliographical details and keywords are printed out for each reference, giving the user enough information to decide which to follow up.

The results of using the KRAS data-base may initially be disconcerting, as pilot searches for staff and students at Leicester have already suggested. To be presented with a list of relevant titles is highly gratifying; to realise that an appreciable number were previously unknown, let alone unread, is less pleasing. The first searches of the data-base may well be followed by a period of industrious reading, giving way gradually to a steady flow of enquiries with occasional large demands prior to the commencement of a new research topic, paper or book. The development of any data-base must be controlled by the needs of the users, and it is intended that KRAS will be developed in close consultation with subscribers. The project will also provide the necessary framework for the fringe subjects of individual card-indexes to be made much more readily available.

The overall result of information exchange on this level can only be an improvement in the standards of research in the discipline. Ultimately the technology which is being developed at present will allow much more comprehensive information retrieval, from complete papers, journals and books stored on computer, and graphical material from video-discs. If the new approach to information services in British archaeology is to realise its full potential, voluntary assistance with dispersed small scale projects will not provide a suitable framework. Standardisation and consistent editorial policy within data-bases are vital, and the important developments in communication between data-bases emphasise the need for careful data definition. The computer networks which are growing at the moment obviate the need for the data-bases themselves to be centralised, but central co-ordination – particularly in the early stages of development – remains essential. It is more efficient to decide on compatibility at the outset, rather than having to spend time later contriving additional software to compensate for the differences between data-bases in a single subject area (Le Maitre, 1981). It seems however that in practice the latter course may be inevitable.

The KRAS project has shown that bibliographical material is a convenient starting-point for the establishment of online data-bases in archaeology. The example of this new type of information service, and the experience gained from it, will prove invaluable as archaeologists begin to take advantage of information technology in other aspects of their discipline.

Bibliography

Amis, P. 1970 An experimental bibliography on science and archaeology. *Science and Archaeology* 1, 20–8
British Library Board 1977 *Problems of information handling in archaeology* British Library Research and Development Report 5329
Celoria, F. S. C. 1971 Some possible search strategies for periodicals relating to archaeology and science. *Science and Archaeology* 5, 31–5
Hasso, M. H. 1978 *A bibliometric study of the literature on archaeology*. unpub. MPhil thesis, Centre for Information Science, City University.

Kempe, D. R. C. 1982 Nature and source of the Gandhara sculptural schist. *Journal of Archaeological Science* 9, 25–8

Le Maitre, J. 1981 SOFIA: a data-base management system applied to archaeology. in Gaines, S. W. *Data-bank Applications in Archaeology* Univ Arizona Press

Le Maitre, J; Lequex, B; Richaud, A–M; Trousson-Liberatore, D. 1980 *Le RIDA. Reseau d'information et de documentation archeologiques; essai de realisation (1974–1979)* Editions ADPF

Miller, F. J. 1974 The structure of the literature of radiocarbon dating: a pilot study of archaeological literature. *Science and Archaeology* 13, 25–34

CHAPTER 10

RETRIEVING INFORMATION FROM COMPUTERISED DATA-BASES: KEYWORDS AND FRANCIS.

J-P. Farruggia

Centre de Documentation Sciences Humaines, Paris

Roger Martlew
Leicester University

Keywording: the nature of the problem.

Roger Martlew

"When he needs what you have gleaned, it is but squeezing you, and, sponge, you shall be dry again" – hamlet IV (ii).

Speed and capacity are usually identified as the factors which make computers particularly suitable for the storage and retrieval of archaeological data. The overall efficiency of a computerised retrieval system, though, lies not so much in the technical specifications – how much a machine can store and how quickly the data can be searched – as in the accuracy with which desired information can be located. This vital aspect has not received much attention in the general excitement over megabytes and nanoseconds. It is the expertise of the people compiling a data-base which will decide whether it is more useful, or more frustrating, than 'old-fasioned' manual systems.

Computers retrieve information by comparing a value entered by the person doing the search with every relevant value in the data-base in turn. The most straightforward case is where a category of information, such as 'pottery type', is identified by a group of characters. These may represent a code, such as 'sam,' or an actual name such as 'samian'; the operator enters 'pottery type' and 'sam', and the computer will compare each record in that category with the retrieval criterion – a process known as string matching. Each time a stored value matches the entered value, the computer records the 'hit' and notes its location. Further instructions will determine how the hits, and any associated information, are displayed on the screen or printer.

This simple description is given in detail because, no matter how complicated the search pattern or how sophisticated the string matching, it is only the ability of the computer to perform this elementary task at high speed which makes it so attractive for information retrieval. The literal 'stupidity' of computers throws responsibility for *efficient* retrieval firmly onto the people who compile and use the data-base: if the computer is given inappropriate values for matching with stored values, it cannot be blamed for producing inadequate results. Similarly, if the stored values do not convey sufficient information, retrieving them accurately will not be of much use. Typing mistakes are the most obvious error, and the most easily corrected; the computer will not know that 'san' should have been 'sam', and will retrieve the wrong data or not score any hits at all. It is more frustrating to try to run a search on a level which is more detailed than the compilers of the data-base allowed for, such as looking for particular forms of samian when only the generic pottery type has been included.

However, with careful planning the problem should be minimal when there is a straightforward, one-to-one relationship between the terms stored on the computer and the information they represent, as in artefact records. Most excavation data-banks or accession catalogues should not therefore present much difficulty in choosing search criteria. With more abstract information, such as would be found in a bibliographical data-base, the choice of key terms is more critical because of different international usage, difficulties of precise definition, and the possibility of using alternative or synonymous terms. It is necessary to establish a classified list or thesaurus of keywords, so that anyone consulting the data-base will be able to discover quickly and easily which terms the computer will 'recognise'. This is discussed in more detail with reference to the KRAS data-base at Leicester (Martlew, this volume).

Compiling a thesaurus is a skilled job, but it is also laborious and time-consuming. Using keywords to identify books and articles is not as exhaustive as indexing, and represents a compromise between the extremes of detailed and general description,. The skill of the person choosing the keywords and the level at which this compromise is reached will determine the accuracy and efficiency of a computerised information retrieval system. Standardisation of terms between different data-bases will obviously make the job easier in the future, but this is an application of information technology which demands wide understanding of the archaeological paradigm, and a logical and carefully-planned approach from the very start. It is a factor which is crucial to the future development of archaeological data-bases, as the present isolation of individual projects is broken down by the rapidly improving communications networks. Official bodies which are already considering this problem, such as the Museum Documentation

Association and the National Monuments Record, need to take a positive lead at this stage to prevent inefficiency and frustration in the future. The following comments by M. J-P Farruggia show that people working in this field are very much aware of the problems which are arising already.

FRANCIS: a bibliographical data-base on archaeology.

J-P Farruggia

CDSH, Paris.

(Translated by M. Ilett)

FRANCIS is the largest on-line data-base in Europe which covers general archaeology. Based in Paris, it is available in this country via the EURONET network and British Telecom's Packet Switching Service. The data-base covers a wide range of bibliographical information, but three sub-files concentrate on archaeology. Numbers 350 and 526 cover European and non-European Art and Archaeology respectively, from the palaeo-Christian era to 1939 for Europe. Sub-file 525 covers world prehistory from the origins of man to the appearance of writing. Methodological publications are also included, as well as articles on human palaeontology and environmental studies (geology, flora and fauna). Multi-disciplinary and social science periodicals received by the Centre de Documentation Sciences Humaines (CDSH) are also checked for articles on prehistory.

Only French prehistory is covered exhaustively: for other countries, the search is limited to journals of national importance produced by major research institutions, museums and universities. A total of four hundred and fifty archaeological journals are checked, to which about two hundred multi-disciplinary periodicals must be added. Most of these are received by the CDSH. A hundred are consulted at the Musée des Antiquités Nationales in Saint Germain en Laye. Books are only considered if they are sent to the CDSH as review copies. However, most books are referred to by means of reviews published in periodicals.

References always include between 1 and 42 keywords, and 65% are accompanied by short abstracts. We use the author's original abstract if this is concise and relevant.

Although the literature consulted comes from all over the world, it can be broken down into the following languages:

French	35%
English	23%
German	15%
Romanic languages	12%
Slav languages	12%

In 1981 English totalled an exceptional 37%. The data-base provides three types of service. A publication, called the 'Bulletin Signalétique', is produced four times a year. This contains the author's index, the index of archaeological sites, the index of cultures, and the subject index. These indexes are made up of the keywords which can be used to interrogate the computer files. Secondly bibliographies in card format, which are used for the selective dissemination of information (SDI). Finally our data-base can be interrogated on-line through Questel-Telesystemes, which is linked to the main international telecommunictions networks such as EURONET.

The problems of keywording FRANCIS

The main difficulty is one of generic and specific keywords: where should the keywording of bibliographical data-bases stop? The happy medium between the few keywords of a traditional subject index and the complex keywording of a data-bank is not easy to establish and is very difficult to maintain in the long term. On first sight the choice of keywords is easy, with combinations such as:

Europe and Germany
Neolithic and Rössen
name of site as given in the text
Grave and Cremation
Lithic and Arrowhead

However, the selection of a limited number of keywords in reality requires analysis and decision. For example we enter Germany but not Bavaria; the French geographical index is more precise (we enter département, commune and name of site). The chronological subdivisions of some prehistoric cultures have keywords (for example la Tène I, La Tène II and La Tène III) as have the subdivisions of major periods (for example Early Neolithic...). Most chronological subdivisions within a culture, though, are not key-worded.

The documentalist's principal task is to convey the author's meaning, but it is not possible to keyword all the information given by an author, for a number of reasons. On FRANCIS the number of keywords is limited to 42, and so keywording does not treat documents in a uniform fashion. A substantial document (for example a long synthetical paper) requires more than 42 keywords. Every short article about a surface scatter of flints can probably be completely described with less than 42. In fact, the less varied the subject matter and the shorter the length of a document, the better it is keyworded! The complete description of a document in keywords can often require time-consuming research (i.e. knowledge of past research, new methodology and critical evaluation), which is impossible for a ducumentalist working alone to undertake. In some rare cases, however, the documentalist will decide not to follow the author's interpretation of a 'hearth', a 'ritual deposit' or a 'posthole'. Although the number of keywords may be small, it is compensated by the ability of the computer to process many different possible combinations. Even with a limited number of keywords it is possible to find a large number of documents.

Nevertheless, my colleagues and I disagree over the problem of the number of keywords. My colleagues, Mdms Labarre and Chardenoux, support the idea of exhaustive keywording. This has the advantage of increasing the accessibility of French literature on prehistory – which is our priority. Furthermore the 'noise', or irrelevant information, which may be retrieved by the combinations of keywords within each document is partly reduced by computer processing, even with documents that treat several cultures (especially in later prehistory), or several themes (such as a congress). The proceedings of a congress can be grouped in a single entry, but the 'noise' generated when this is retrieved can be reduced if each conference paper is treated as a separate document. Exhaustive keywording is also the most suitable way of preparing for future use of the data-base, since it is extremely difficult and inefficient to go back through the data-base at a later stage to insert additional keywords.

To conclude, the number of keywords depends largely on the documentalist's judgement. This important responsibility must be shared with the researchers who use the data-base.

CHAPTER 11

FORTY YEARS OF INFORMATION COLLECTION BY THE COUNCIL FOR BRITISH ARCHAEOLOGY

Cherry Lavell

Council for British Archaeology

Although annual compilations of some sort have been made for British archaeology for most years since the 1880s (Gomme, 1912, preface; CBA, 1949, preface), it was only after the formation of the Council for British Archaeology (replacing the old Congress of Archaeological Societies) in 1944 that a firm and continuous base for systematic bibliography became available. The first issue of the *Archaeological Bulletin for the British Isles* covered the war years 1940–46 and appeared in 1949. The format devised then, by Molly Cotton and Florence Patchett, has continued to this day with little change. Individual entries have tended to grow in size as excavations became more complex, however, and a subject index to the whole compilation was added starting with the 1950–51 issue. That same issue, 1950–51, saw the cessation of attempts to include unpublished finds and a consequent change of title to the more explicit and accurate *Archaeological Bibliography for Great Britain and Ireland*.

Undoubtedly the addition of the subject index was a great improvement, since it added a third 'entry route', and a badly needed one, to the two which already gave access to the Bibliography entries – the county arrangement and the authors' list. However, the layout of the publication could have done with more careful planning, since a researcher starting with the subject entry – querns, say – was faced with three stages of looking up. Under 'querns' one found some page references; on each of those pages one had to find the actual entry; against each entry was a number which referred to the appropriate item in the author list. How much better it would have been had the 'querns' entry led straight to the author list! Even so, however cumbrous was the process, the Bibliography was doing a great deal of the researcher's work for him; it was covering the publications of all the national and county societies, together with many of the smaller publications (as long as they were 'properly' printed and not cyclostyled). In the early years of the Bibliography there were 83 national and county/local publications. Many researchers setting out on a topic new to them would automatically turn to the Bibliography as by far the quickest means of scanning the literature. After all, for a 10-year search, nobody would relish the job of handling 500 or 600 individual issues to be scanned page by page (or, more recklessly, by contents list alone) when a mere 10 volumes of Bibliography would do the job for them.

How reliable was the Bibliography ? As far as I know no one has ever done a full bibliometric study of it; but I believe that, although most people would claim to have found at least a couple of references that the Bibliography had missed, it probably provides at least 90–95% of the total available references on any given subject. The authors' list would tend to be rather better than that, since any omissions in the Bibliography as a whole are more likely to arise through insufficient depth of analysis than through the omission of entire articles.

What do people look for? Again we are very much in the dark about how the Bibliography is used, though numerous people have told us they use it as a back-up to ensure that they have found everything needed. And, as I said earlier, many people use it to find their way into a new topic.

It has to be admitted that there are certain areas from which the Bibliography has always tended to shy away. For instance, successive editors have accepted a convention that books and monographs do not receive the same depth of analysis as articles. (This was all right in the relaxed days when the publication of a whole book on an archaeological topic was a relatively rare event so that it was difficult to avoid hearing about it.) Another area where the Bibliography has probably fallen short is in 'scientific' archaeology: bits of charcoal, animal bones, and laboratory processes like thermoluminescence dating have all been gathered together in the subject index under the single heading 'scientific aids' which would tend to diminish their individual importance. Nor was any material later than AD 1600 treated, so that industrial archaeology was left to fend for itself, as were Victorian buildings or 18th century wig-curlers; to be sure, embarking on those fields would need more staff time than has ever been available. Perhaps more serious still was the fact that the Bibliography scan was always confined within these shores so that material published abroad for any reason was not included in the Bibliography, no matter how important it was.

By about 1965, and certainly by 1970, these deficiencies were beginning to become serious; but the successive Bibliography editors (who were all part-time voluntary workers, albeit with considerable archaeological know-ledge) were always cramped for time. It was always a scramble to round up the last few stray articles for any given year, especially when local journals or even national ones could be up to two years late in appearing. With the immense rise in the amount of excavation from 1972 onwards, there came an inevitable (if time-lagged) increase in the numbers of publications to be scanned. There were by this time over 200 journals dealing partly or wholly with archaeology in existence, and numbers of books were increasing too. Not only this, but the excavations themselves were becoming enormously more complex and the amount of information recorded in reports was correspondingly more difficult and time-consuming to analyse (Rahtz, 1974, 19; Fowler, 1977, 169–72; Lavell, 1981a, 108). Hence the Bibliography has begun to lag further and further behind the works it analyses, and is currently running five years late. A period like that is long enough for an archaeological theory to come in and go out again, and these delays are accordingly a souce of great concern within the CBA as well as outside it (British Library, 1977).

Computerisation would assist to some extent, but the principal need is for extra staff time to conduct the analyses and get them into print in a timely fashion. It cannot be too strongly stressed that indexing of archaeological material is a highly skilled job (Lavell, 1981b) and that volunteer help with the analyses can sometimes be a mixed blessing. The work needs a wide knowledge of archaeology, from palaeolithic to post-medieval; it needs extreme accuracy, consistency in application, and above all dedication to an essentially unattractive task.[1] In a commercial subject like chemical engineering, or one with Government interest behind it like atomic physics, the flow of information can be quantified in economic terms and extra staff funded when necessary. Not so in archaeology; as far back as 1908 the annual index of archaeological papers was making a loss, and the archaeological community has never supported its information services with sufficient enthusiasm to ensure proper funding (Congress of Archaeological Societies, 1913, 2–3; O'Neil, 1946, 61–2; Lavell, 1981a, 110–12). The band of workers who find the Bibliography indispensable to their research is not large enough by itself to ensure viability, and the Bibliography print run has only been kept to a workable level by including the publication in a subscription package along with other CBA periodicals. This is remaining true even when the number of items indexed annually has now risen to over 2000, or double what it was in the early 1970s. One is driven to ask how people manage to keep up with their subjects in these conditions without recourse to the Bibliography!

Is there perhaps a philosophical point here: that a centralised information service like the CBA's cannot now hope to satisfy the increasingly specialised needs of its public? Is this why one sees the appearance here and there of client-centred services like the University of Leicester Department of Archaeology's scheme currently under development for worldwide information on scientific archaeology, or the computerisation of county sites-and-monuments records? If the CBA were to develop a jumbo computerised bibliography would it fill the needs of today's archaeological community? We would be glad to hear from our potential users! Since we have so far failed to obtain funds for our own computer to help us compile a more sophisticated combination of Abstracts and Bibliography (British Library, 1977) we are currently looking for an extant computerised set-up into which we could slot ourselves[2]. It will be surprising if any of these has the depth of indexing capacity required in the bibliography up to now; for instance, the prehistoric section of the French *Bulletin Signalétique (525)* has only 42 indexing fields, whereas the Bibliography often has needed twice as many as that.

Maybe archaeologists will have to be content with asking broader questions: instead of asking what 9-post structures have been found, for instance, the question might have to be framed as 'what timber structures'; rather than ask for Viking bone combs, the researcher may need to be content with Migration period bone objects. The search work, in other words, may have to be passed back to the researcher just when he was hoping to have it done even more specifically for him. It will all come down to funds in the end: is the archaeological community prepared to fight for the staff and the equipment needed to keep its information flowing? If not, more and more individuals will have to spend more and more time leafing through countless journals. Nobody could think that an efficient use of time.

Notes

1. A recent French experiment in archaeological bibliography failed because the specialists who were meant to index articles in their own fields found the job altogether too tedious. (Le Maître *et al*, 1980, 68)

2. Since this paper was written the purchase of a CBA computer has come much nearer, but its availability for bibliographic work remains in doubt, as priority will be given to financial management tasks.

Bibliography

British Library 1977 Problems of information handling in archaeology: report of a seminar, *Brit Lib Res & Devel Rep*, 5329.
CBA 1949 *Archaeological bulletin for the British Isles 1940–46*, Council for British Archaeology
Congress of Archaeological Societies 1913 Report for 1913
Fowler, P.J. 1977 *Approaches to archaeology*
Gomme, A. 1912 *Index to archaeological papers published in 1908*, Congress of Archaeological Societies
Lavell, C. 1981a Publication: an obligation, *Bull Inst Archaeol Univ London*, 18, 91–125
Lavell, C. 1981b Problems of archaeological indexing, *The Indexer*, 12(4), 175–84
Le Maître, J. *et al* 1980 *Le RIDA: réseau d'information et de documentation archéologiques: essai de réalisation* (Paris)
O'Neil, B. H. St J. 1946 The Congress of Archaeological Societies, *Antiq J.*, 26, 61–6
Rahtz, P. 1974 In Grinsell, Leslie, *et al, The preparation of archaeological reports*

CHAPTER 12

COST EFFECTIVE PUBLISHING

Alan Sutton

Alan Sutton Publishing Limited

There are many arguments amongst archaeologists about what to publish and how to present their publications. There are arguments about time – compilers' time, and now even more – readers' time.

Some say that from the published account it should be possible to reconstruct the site on paper, and that it should be possible from the report to judge the quality of the excavations and the skill of the excavator. Whatever the requirements are, and how they are formulated is a matter for the professional archaeologist to judge, but how the information reaches its audience is a completely separate matter.

In the nineteenth century there was only one major method of disseminating information apart from the spoken word, and that was letterpress printing. During the twentieth century many new forms of information dissemination have become available, including broadcasting which is now by far the largest dispenser of information in relation to numbers reached. However, for specialist information, the more traditional methods persist, merely utilizing spin-offs from the technological boom. These include the simple use of the typewriter linked with an ordinary office duplicator, photocopiers, microfilm and microfiche. Some of these, or a combination of all of these, can be used to disseminate the information for a very modest sum, but with so much paper bombarding us every day, yet another batch of A4 paper stapled together, with a microfiche taped onto the back sheet, may not get a fair reception; unless of course the recipient is eagerly waiting to absorb every word. Even if it is urgently wanted, typescript is not easy to read and concentrate upon. It is far easier to read the printed word in a book. Somehow the originator has to present the information in a manner he can afford, in a way in which the recipient can easily absorb and actually wishes to pay for. Therefore, we must be talking of some form of attractive, well presented publication, leaving aside for the moment the pros and cons of microfiche.

There has been a great deal of discussion about word-processors amongst the more technologically minded; about how useful it would be to key the initial reports, alter them, correct them, rearrange them and then send the floppy disk for photosetting. This would obviate much of the odious proof-reading and cut out the largest single constituent element in the cost of printing – keyboard entry. Although this does have great possibilities for the future there are still many problems to overcome, not least of which is the proliferation of different types of word-processor and photosetting interfaces.

The technology is now available, and in many similar applications is actually working. Some large publishers have been toying with the idea of editing text on their own word-processors and sending disks to their printers for photosetting. At present the N.G.A. objection to non-union source material is very real, and from the Unions' position understandable. Many hot-metal compositors are currently unemployed, having been superseded by the revolutionary typesetting changes of the last fifteen years. However, through a partially changing attitude, possibly because the floodgates of progress cannot be barricaded and held tight, new opportunities are arising. At present, material keyed on tape or cassette is acceptable without the key depressions having been union originated. More exciting is the acceptance in some areas of non-union source material supplied on floppy disk providing that the editing is handled by an N.G.A. compositor. Using machines currently available this should not be a drawback, as most word-processors do not have compatible codes for photosetting, and require manual intervention anyway.

Incompatibility is still a major stumbling block, but even before this book is published, new developments will make opportunities available for many word-processor owners. The front-ending of new photosetting units has been revolutionized, and some manufacturers are realizing that coding their machines to be unique is lessening sales of their relatively expensive photosetting units rather than enhancing sales of their own keyboards. An example of this is the new arrangement made between Linotype Paul Limited and Apple. Apple now make micro-computers compatible with their existing range which they pass to Linotype Paul for the addition of the Linotype keyboard with the photosetting command keys. This very successful tie-up has led to other photosetting machinery manufacturers looking for similar arrangements in the microprocessor market. Although exciting, this still does not completely solve the standardization problem but 70% compatability is certainly possible.

Fig. 5 shows how a conventional typesetting department may be run at a large book printing house. The example is for a photosetting unit provided by the market leader, Linotype Paul, and a typical unit is the Linotron 202, a powerful digital machine which formulates characters from 4 point to 72 point on a minute dot matrix system utilizing fibre optics (see Fig. 6). The keyboards and mainframe computer may have been designed for the printer to offer him specific page make-up facilities. The example shows nine keyboards sending data to the mainframe, front-ending the photosetting unit. This is an in-house keyboard installation, and to all intents and purposes acts in the same way as an old letterpress installation inasmuch as the only acceptable input medium is a typescript.

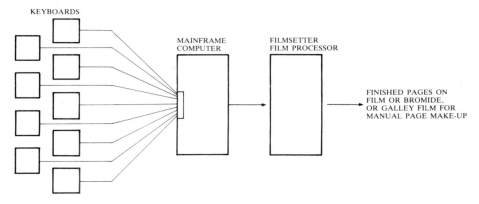

Fig. 5

Even with the proliferation of manufacturers of micro-computers and word-processors, some limited standardization is available by specialist computer houses who can take any form of tape and disk and by using a custom built 'black box' amend it to read any form of header label by a switching process. This form of specialist ability is not yet common, but in the near future, all printers wishing to remain in the mainstream of typesetting and origination will need to be able to take disks from four or five different makes of machine. Some of these printers will possibly operate a modem system through the telephone network. At location A, a university department for example, a disk reader (or possibly the micro-computer/word-processor itself) will be connected to a telephone modem. A quick telephone call to any printer having a modem on the same coding structure will enable the contents of the disk to be copied down the line for compositor editing. A possible photosetting set-up at the printer (location B) is as shown in Fig. 6. This shows a reduced internal keyboard capability with a mix of input; customers' disks received in the post, customers' disk contents received by telephone and the traditional typescript. The editing terminal would be used to read a client's disk, possibly sent as raw data. The editor's machine would read the data, probably stop on meeting a code that it did not recognize, and the editor would insert the relevant photosetting codes. These can include a large variety of phonetics and superior numbers, as well as the basic instructions for point size, weight of type and spacing information.

Another area where considerable research and development has been made over the last decade is OCR – optical character recognition. At one time it was thought that OCR offered the best way forward, but in recent times it has fallen behind its more versatile technological cousin – the micro-computer with its superior ability to capture data. OCR also requires

117

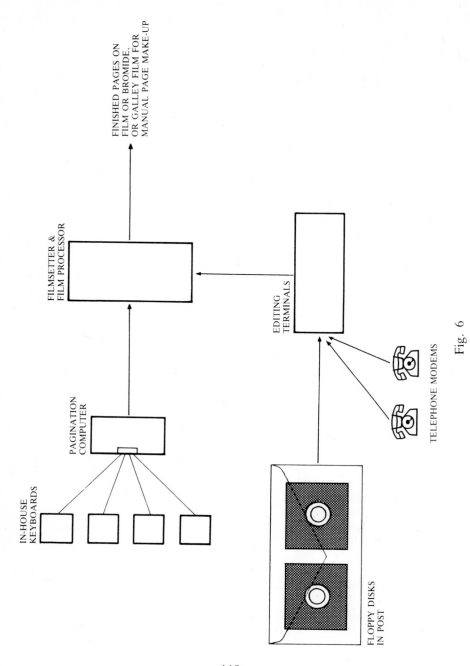

IN-HOUSE
KEYBOARDS

PAGINATION
COMPUTER

FILMSETTER &
FILM PROCESSOR

FINISHED PAGES ON
FILM OR BROMIDE,
OR GALLEY FILM FOR
MANUAL PAGE MAKE-UP

EDITING
TERMINALS

TELEPHONE MODEMS

FLOPPY DISKS
IN POST

Fig. 6

118

a special typewriter or, at best, recognizes only a limited range of typewriters. The problem of handwritten symbols slowing the input by continually flagging them as errors means that any alteration to a typescript must be kept to a minimum. Therefore, instead of alterations being carried out by the author/contributor as an annotation on the typescript, they are invariably left until first proof stage to be added as an author correction. Although applications for OCR will continue, the main way forward must be with data capture.

While we all practice with these new systems, and learn to use micro-computers to ease and assist the job we have in hand – for archaeologists building data-bases, bibliographical references and quick information re-trieval; for printers using new computerized dot matrix photosetting equipment – we should look carefully at the current costs of production and see how, through being more efficient, these costs can be brought down. With computers, or any machines, there is only one way to operate, and that is the correct way. Any incorrect code or mis-keyed information will throw the system. Unlike the human compositor who can actually make a decision, or at least question an instruction, the computer is quite heartless and will throw it all back in an utter jumble with no apology at all. What is often not appreciated is that by giving a mess of a typescript to a printer with the understanding that 'he will sort it out', it is actually costing a great deal of money. There are not many computerized keyboards for typesetting costed below £20 an hour, and yet some authors and editors are prepared to send in copy with only general and rather vague instructions regarding style. This lack of direction often applies to a typescript that has been prepared on a dozen different typewriters, has been edited several times and contains annotations, additions and deletions. Typesetting on an average archaeological journal, sewn limp bound of which 1,000 are printed, is usually more than 60% of the total cost to the customer; yet this can be reduced considerably, giving a real saving to any customer. All that is needed is forethought and the discipline that we are prepared to give to a computer.

For a non-printer it is not easy to visualize how a set piece of text will look from a set of instructions such as 'Times Roman over 30 picas, 10/12, headings in 16 point upper and lower bold ranged left followed by 6 points of space'! And yet this type of detailed instruction enables a compositor to key at full speed without the need for calculating the type of heading or subheading required or whether text should be indented, etc. It reduces the expensive author's corrections and speeds the progress to the finished publication.

The style set should ideally be well known to all contributors in the team. It saves a great deal of editorial time if everyone is using the same house style. This applies most of all in archaeology to the forms of punctuation or abbreviation, and of course to the form of abbreviations themselves, but there are also the minor considerations such as spelling out numbers up to twenty or one hundred, and the forms that dates should take. If these slip through on final copy, it will cost dearly as, even with new technology, author's corrections are extremely expensive.

The explanations and descriptions of the new technology machinery now available for typesetting have been leading up to the main point of this paper; how the new facilities can be utilized for the publication of archaeological reports. It is unfortunate to see the number of books sent for printing which have not been given a detailed structural plan from conception through to the finished typescript. By following a simple check-list it is possible to provide the printer with a typescript that is going to proceed smoothly through the press with the minimum of time and effort. By not following the check-list it may prove costly if an author correction is needed, or if it is realized at the last moment that the standardizing of headings has not been followed! The check-list given below is by no means exhaustive; however, it may be of considerable value to archaeologists unfamiliar with editorial duties who find themselves delegated to see a report through the press.

1. Choose a house style for contributors to follow, noting particularly the style you are adopting for abbreviations. Specify also a ruling on the style of headings. Each heading should be listed in order of importance A, B, C, D, etc. On the style sheet for house style given to each contributor, denote how the headings and sub-headings will be printed, i.e. A, will be large caps. centred; B, will be small caps. ranged left; C, will be text size upper and lower italics ranged left; (these are obviously examples only). The style sheet should perhaps denote that the correct way of showing these on the typescript are: large caps. – treble underlined; small caps. – double underlined; italics – single underlined. The CBA leaflet entitled *Signposts for Archaeological Publication* offers a very useful set of standards for style and layout.

2. Specify to all contributors the regime being adopted for presentation of typescript. Ideally this should be sixty-five characters per line (including bar spaces) by thirty-one lines deep, double spaced. This gives an average 2,000 key depressions per typescript page (approx. 334 words). Therefore, every three pages of typescript will equate to 1,000 words. It is a simple matter to discover the size of typewriter each contributor is using, they fall into three main categories; ten, eleven or twelve characters per inch. By the editor supplying contributors with the paper to use for their typescript, with four vertical lines (see Fig. 7), the editor can ensure that at all times he is keeping an accurate eye on the extent for each contribution.

3. Specify to all contributors the form of notation to be included on all illustrations, line drawings or half-tones. The simplest tag is the contributor's surname followed by plate X, or fig. X; e.g. Jones: fig. 23. Where a volume is to have integral illustrations and text, the position for the illustration should be marked in the margin of the typescript and galley-proofs. On page make-up the illustration will

A4 SHEET
WITH 4 VERTICAL
LINES FOR
DUPLICATING PRIOR
TO DESPATCH TO
CONTRIBUTORS

LINE 1 = LEFT HAND
        MARGIN
LINE 2 = 65 BAR SPACES
        ON 12 CHAR. TO
        INCH MACHINE
LINE 3 = 65 BAR SPACES
        ON 11 CHAR. TO
        INCH MACHINE
LINE 4 = 65 BAR SPACES
        ON 10 CHAR. TO
        INCH MACHINE

A = STARTING POINT
B = 31 LINES DOUBLE
    SPACED

Fig. 7

then be placed at the nearest suitable point. Illustrations should also be carefully identified with an identical tag and a reduction size. Any half-tone which includes an area to be cropped should be supplied with a tracing paper overlay with the cropped area marked. Supplying the half-tone with the crop area on the back is unsuitable.

4. Captions for all illustrations should be supplied on separate sheets of A4 paper as well as on the drawings themselves.

5. Ensure that towards the final stages duplicate typescripts are in existence.

6. Decide upon the format for the publication, A4 (297mm x 210mm), Crown Quarto (246mm x 186mm) or some other size. Photocopy a page from a journal that is closest to the style aimed for and send it with the typescript to the printers when seeking quotations and when placing work.

7. Decide upon the smallest quantity that a quotation is required for. Decide upon the quality of paper required; for an integrally illustrated volume, the ideal paper stock is a matt cartridge of 115gsm (the same quality and weight that this volume is printed on).

8. Select four printers for test quotations. It is better to choose printers used to book work, especially archaeological journals. At this point do *not* send the typescript, but send a list of points as follows:-

Please supply a quotation *not* an estimate for producing the following publication entitled ...., for which a type-script and illustrations will be available on ★★/★★/★★.

Print run xxxx copies. Please quote per hundred run-on also.
Trim size xxxmm x xxxmm.
Extent of typescript xxx pp.
Total number of words (see attached sheet for article or chapter breakdown).
Complexity of setting as sample typescript (*send spare photocopy of a typical page of typescript*).
Style requested similar to sample finished page (*send spare photocopy of the style aimed for*).
Number of line illustrations xx. xxx full page/xxx half page/xx fold outs.
Number of half-tones xxx full page /xxx half page.
Style of binding required (sewn limp or full cased).
Style of cover required (specify if jacket for cased volume or cover for sewn-limp bound volume, stipulate cover material for jacket to be not less than 115gsm, and for sewn-limp cover to be not less than 240gsm. Always specify how many colours are required, and if full colour that a transparency will be supplied. Always stipulate that the jacket/cover must be laminated.
Type of paper .... (*ask for sample also*).

Number of proof stages required ....

Number of proof sets for each stage ....

Delivery address ....

It is worthwhile ensuring that no extra charges will accrue, including delivery, and worthwhile asking what the charges are per mark for author corrections. If offprints are required, the charges for these should also be established during test quote stage.

9. With the test quote the printer should also be asked about the forms of disk that he can accept in case any of the volume is submitted as such. When all test quotes are in, the lowest two should be selected for sending the live typescript in turn for an actual cast-off and quotation.

10. Now the exciting stage: committing the volume to print. After deciding upon the quotation to accept, tie up the loose ends. Ensure that the typescript to be submitted is final and conforms in all ways to the house style that was initially specified. Then tie the printer to an agreed schedule and a fixed quotation agreed by exchange of letters. Ensure that the quotation received does not leave the printer leeway to add trade increases as long as the schedule is not broken on your side. A suggested schedule for an average length archaeological report or county journal is as follows:-

Origination to galley stage – six weeks

Galley or page on galley proofing by client – four weeks

Correcting and submitting page proofs – four weeks

Final checking by client and submitting index copy – three weeks

Setting index and final corrections – two weeks

Index proofing by client – one week

Correcting index and preparing for print – two weeks

Printing – six weeks

Binding – four weeks

There are several other points that could be made, but space here does not allow for an exhaustive description of the modern printing processes and how to get the most out of them. There are just two points which are worth raising and which cannot be stressed too much. Firstly, do not continually bombard your printer with notes, pedantic little points and annoying telephone calls. If he is a competent book printer he will know how to produce your book for you. Constant calls and notes are more likely to create a disaster rather than avoid one. If there are any amendments to make or points relating to the text that you wish to raise mark them on the proofs not as a postscript to one of many letters! Remember that the person dealing with the delivery of your books will not necessarily be the compositor setting the type and any letter dealing with different points in this way can create problems. Secondly, act professionally even if you are not a professional. If you are delegated to spend several thousand pounds on producing a book, remember to spend the time going through the check-list shown above, and read other books available on the subject of book production. When you get the proofs, ensure that you have three sets, one for the contributor, one for yourself, and one to collate all the marks on. On the collated set mark printer's errors in red and author corrections in blue or black. Do not try to cover up author corrections by slipping them in as red and hoping to get away with it. It is painfully obvious to a compositor what is and what is not his or her error and the only thing that the client will gain is a sense of ill-feeling on the part of the compositor who feels maligned! Treat this first set of proofs as *the* set of proofs, and do not rely on skimping through the first set hoping to pick up errors you have missed on the second. The second proof pass should be used *only* to check that the corrections specified have been actioned, to add page references, and as basis for the index. Many of the comments made above will appear as absolutely obvious, but it is amazing how much money can be wasted by ignoring the obvious.

In the first part of this paper we have seen how new technology can reduce origination costs by the capture of key depressions at the initial stage of typescript. In the second part we have seen how through careful organization at the preparation stage we can reduce production costs. Now we come to the matter of microfiche. This is a thorny problem and one that I feel ill-qualified to comment upon. Obviously they have great value in reducing costs, but what about the aesthetics? It is pointless to argue that the price per page for 1000 printed copies is £20.00 and the price per page for 1000 fiche is only £2.00 when the most costly element is left out on the fiche figure – the origination. It seems to be acceptable to photograph typescript for use on a microfiche, whereas for the printed word it has to be typeset for aesthetic reasons. If the same medium of typescript was used for the printed version as well as the fiche, the difference could be drastically reduced. The printed version would come down to about £7.00 per page as against the microfiche at £2.00! Take this one stage further. If four pages of A4 typescript were photoreduced by 50% (still perfectly legible) and placed as a group of four pages on one A4 printed page this would bring the price down to about £4.00 per page. Although still twice as expensive as microfiche it does have the advantage of being visible without the aid of a reader. There is no reason why a volume should not be a mixture of typeset and typewritten text.

Finally, a word or two about paper. Without a doubt the best paper for use on integrally illustrated volumes is the matt coated cartridge mentioned earlier. In the letterpress era, art paper was very popular for printing plates, and many still prefer it today but it is much more costly than the matt cartridge. This is not because of the paper itself – art paper is more or less the same cost as coated cartridge. However, art paper cannot easily be used on the process of 'perfecting', that is the printing of both sides of the sheet in one pass. Most larger printers have perfecting presses that can print a 64 page section in one pass through the machine, 32 pages on each side. Art paper takes longer for the ink to dry and therefore is not the easiest of papers to 'perfect' on. Printing is now a highly automated process, and any process that reduces the job from being straightforward increases the cost considerably. Any job that is an 'even working' of 32 page sections is going to be most cost beneficial. Any job that has oddments plus art paper sections, and possibly tips of over-large drawings, will be the most costly!

New developments in origination and printing are being announced all the time. Within a very few years I shall read through this paper and think how very naive I was to reach some of the conclusions shown above. However, before technology makes me and my livelihood completeley redundant, I hope that some of the points above will be of help in making archaeological reports cost-effective.

CHAPTER 13

PUBLISHING IN THE ELECTRONIC AGE: AN OVERVIEW OF DEVELOPMENT IN THE PUBLISHING INDUSTRY

David Powell

Longman Group Ltd

Since I am not an archaeologist and since most of what I know about the subject has been acquired listening to the papers preceding my own at this conference, I feel quite justified in taking you away from archaeology for a while. Nevertheless, I am sure you will find that what is happening in the publishing industry is of interest and relevance to you in archaeology.

I propose to divide my paper into three parts, dealing first with recent events in the publishing industry, moving on to a consideration of the wide range of electronic media now available to us, and concluding with a brief discussion of some of the principal issues which are raised by the development of the new media.

The publishing industry is now beginning to take 'new technology' seriously. Although only a small number of publishers are actively marketing – as opposed to developing or experimenting with – publications using the new media, two very signifiant steps have been taken within the last twelve months or so.

Firstly, a major new association was founded in early 1981, the International Electronic Publishing Research Centre (IEPRC). It got off to a good start, with the first meeting of its Board of Management at the House of Lords in London on 9 April 1981 and the first meeting of its Research Committee at the European Commission building in Luxembourg on 1 June 1981. It has already attracted a fair number of members from most of the major countries of Western Europe. Research projects are already getting under way, most notably a ten-year forecast of development in electronic publishing, which is expected to give members of IEPRC valuable insights into current and future trends in this field together with comment on economic, technological and social factors likely to encourage or hinder progress. Additionally, there is to be work on the standardization of character sets with a view to moving towards a common input language. In association with Publishers' Databases Limited (see below) and the European Commission, a study of user needs and technology options for an electronic document delivery system has just been completed.

Secondly, a number of publishers, brought together through participation in the UK Publishers Association Electronic Publishing Panel, recently agreed to form a new company, called Publishers' Databases Limited (PDL). A key principle underlying the formation of PDL is that it should be an "open access" company. Any publishing firm may, therefore, join the consortium and provisions have been included in the Articles of Association which will prevent any single company, or even a small clique, from gaining overall control.

Whereas IEPRC is a research organization, PDL is a commercial venture dedicated to the profitable application of the new technology, although it is recognised by all members that profitability is a long-term objective. This is not to say that PDL would not fund or sponsor specific research, but its emphasis is on application and exploitation. PDL is a notable example of members of an industry getting together to do jointly what individual members – particularly the smaller ones – would have difficulty in undertaking alone.

IEPRC and PDL will clearly be complementary organizations. Indeed, as noted above, they have already worked together, in conjunction with the European Commission, on a technical feasibility study matching user needs and technology options for a document delivery system (i.e. a system permitting electronic search and retrieval of full text, with a hard-copy print-out facility, if required, either at the user end or offline, at a remote centre, for subsequent forwarding). This technical study is, in fact, the logical successor to a market feasibility study which had been completed earlier for the PA Electronic Publishing Panel and which had established that there would be a market demand for such a service.

Finally in Information Technology Year, it is worth noting that the Department of Industry has sponsored work on an electronic mail system and possible document delivery system based on a particular medium, namely teletex (in layman's terms a very sophisticated version of telex, with a much wider character set and supported by computers and telecommunications networks – not to be confused with the broadcast teletext systems). This work, under the name Project Hermes, is intended ultimately to stimulate UK manufacture of the hardware.

I should like to give some attention now to the media, and to clarify the term "electronic publishing".

Publishing is not about the printed word and only the printed word; it is the acquisition, organization and dissemination of material – that is, literally, "making public". The medium employed is not the prime consideration, although it should be expected that a good publisher would

127

select the most apropriate medium for any material to be made public.

In the last 10–20 years, the range of publishing media has widened considerably. Some of the main developments have been described in the paper by John Wilcock (Chapter 2). The pace of technology means that it is necessary to keep a close watch on developments and continually to assess and review a dynamic situation. Progress is steadily reducing the constraints associated with some of the new media. A number of trends or areas of development which appear to be significant, in addition to those mentioned by Wilcock, deserve to be highlighted.

Printing and publishing technology can no longer be considered separately from what is sometimes referred to disparagingly as "office technology". No distinction can or should be made. In particular, the whole of the broad areas of word processing and facsimile transmission may not be set aside. Difficulties undoubtedly exist because of lack of standardisation and compatibility, but the problems are being reduced and will certainly be overcome in the foreseeable future.

Free-language searching of full-text data-banks has already been with us for some years, most notably with the Lexis and Nexis services set up by Mead Data Central in the USA. More and more full-text data-banks will become available.

In the last few years there has been some particularly interesting experimentation with the so-called "electronic journal". An important initiative in this field was undertaken at the New Jersey Institute of Technology, between 1976 and 1980. Despite results which were, on the face of it, somewhat depressing, a lot was learnt about the effect of technical factors on human interest and motivation. Since British participation in that experiment was, at quite a late stage in the preparations, effectively blocked by the Post Office, the cause was embraced in the UK by the British Library, which has funded a major $3\frac{1}{2}$ year research project at the Universities of Birmingham and Loughborough. BLEND (Birmingham and Loughborough Electronic Network Development) was set up to conduct all the functions of a journal, including authorship, refereeing, editing and reading via computer terminals and networks. Appropriately enough, the subject of this journal is "computer human factors". The experiment is now at about its half-way point, since it was intended to be online for 3 years from 1 January 1981. Full information can be obtained from Professor B. Shackel at the Department of Human Sciences at Loughborough.

With a much wider range of media available, we must expect to see more mixed media publishing. Materials will tend to be disseminated in the medium or media which is/are most suited to the nature of the content and the market to be reached (see Hassall, this volume). Hitherto, whilst the logic of such an approach may have been accepted, the means have not really been available to put it into practice.

The implications of information technology
We are all familiar with the fundamental chicken and egg issue: users are

reluctant to invest in hardware unless a certain amount of data are available, whereas it is pointless creating a data-bank which is not going to receive use. Although of considerable importance now, this problem is essentially temporary. How long it will take for the problem to resolve itself and whether we are able to influence the time scale are important, but difficult supplementary questions. There are, however, two encouraging facts. Firstly, we know that costs – both of equipment and of use – are, in real terms, static or coming down. Secondly, we know that the rate of growth, however measured, is high. For example, estimates of the value of the world market for online access to bibliographic data-bases and factual data-banks vary – one credible source put it at around $ 1 billion for 1980 – but there is a reasonable degree of agreement that growth is in the region of 25–40% per annum.

For any organisation proposing to set up and manage any sort of electronic information service, careful consideration of the design of the system is essential. It is important at the outset to have a clear idea of objectives and to pay close attention to users' information, software and hardware needs. This statement may seem self-evident. It is, after all, no more than we should be doing anyway. But with any sort of electronic system there is no room for vague or sloppy thinking. An analytical approach is vital, as well as an appreciation of how to cope with the inexorable logic of the computer.

Input is a much discussed problem, but with the spread of word-processors and micro- and mini-computers and other devices, such as Optical Character Recognition readers which work at high speed from ordinary typescript, the technical difficulties are diminishing. If something is to be typeset or typed, then, for relatively little extra expense, a method can be used which will simultaneously generate a magnetic medium. Such facilities do not, however, dispense with the need to edit and structure data carefully and to monitor quality and maintain consistency. If anything, the need is greater than ever, although for larger jobs with standard formats input 'menus' or 'prompts' can be very helpful. The technical problems of compatibility and interfacing are also being overcome and we can look forward with confidence to the day when transferability from floppy disc to mainframe will be easy.

Access and retrieval remain of paramount importance. Whatever the technical aids we have, we are, nevertheless, imprisoned by the limitations of our own language. Free-language or 'fuzzy' searching facilities will not substitute for good indexing in a lot of academic disciplines. Our language frequently lacks precision, usage is inconsistent, words are ambiguous and there are too many synonyms – or apparent synonyms. The indexer will not disappear, although his/her role may be modified. Cherry Lavell's call for a "common thesaurus of archaeological terms" in a recent article is not misplaced (Lavell, 1981).

In conclusion, I believe all of us have heard predictions by some commentators of the 'paperless society'. That is conceivable, but only just, and it is a long way off yet. But the central point is that a very different communications society is in formation, after 500 years or so with few fundamental changes. Outlooks and attributes will have to change and the key to the future, as Dr. Henry Cleere said in the opening paper, lies in education and training.

Bibliography
Lavell, C 1981 Problems of archaeological indexing. *The Indexer* 12(4), 175–84

CHAPTER 14

THE DEPARTMENT OF THE ENVIRONMENT VIEW OF CURRENT TRENDS IN PUBLICATION

Pamela V. Clarke

Post-Excavation/Publication Section:

Inspectorate of Ancient Monuments and Historic Buildings

Most people are aware that it is possible for the Department of the Environment to provide grant-aid for archaeological publication. Fewer seem aware however of the statutory considerations which govern the Department's archaeological role. Its main function is the preservation of monuments. Where mounments of national importance cannot be preserved by one of the other means open to it, the Department may support archaeological excavation and investigation, in order that some form of record of those monuments may be preserved. The primary function of the Department is not to support academic research as such but, of course, the recording of threatened sites does add considerably to our knowledge of the past. Research objectives therefore figure in the selection of sites for investigation, and archaeological work on those monuments which are in the Department's care also contributes to historical scholarship. In supporting preservation by record the Department has over the years become increasingly involved both in ensuring that the results of excavations are published and in the means of publication.

Growth in volume of publications

Archaeological activities have grown considerably in scale, scope and complexity over the past twenty-five years and an ever-widening range of skills and techniques has been developed during this time in order to extract more and more detailed information.

This complexity originated in changes in on-site recording techniques with the increased use of pro-forma, (eg Jefferies 1977 fig. 2 p. 20). This type of detailed and co-ordinated recording involves time consuming post-excavation processing which can involve rather mechanistic and boring work. The fully recorded excavation report produced can be very difficult to read, although many of the recent examples do in fact take the Pitt-Rivers publication format (Pitt Rivers 1887–98) to its logical conclusion given modern techniques.

Not only have excavation methods increased in scale and complexity, there has also been an increase in the number of excavations taking place. An analysis of the '*Excavations, Annual Reports*' published by the Department (MPBW 1956–61 HMSO 1962–76) shows the Department's growing involvement in rescue excavation (see Fig. 8).

In 1956, there were 55 rescue excavations and 25 publications recorded, a ratio of 2.2:1.

In 1966 there were 134 rescue excavations, and 36 publications recorded, a ratio of 4:1.

In 1976, 309 rescue excavations were recorded and 86 pubblications recorded, a ratio of 3.6:1.

The figures quoted above are derived from the summaries of excavations published each year in these annual reports. They are intended to give a general picture only of the scale of grant aid to rescue excavation by the Department. They do not include excavations which may have taken place, but for which no summary was supplied by the excavator, excavations on the Department's guardianship sites, research excavations carried out by other bodies, or any other work which did not involve Departmental expenditure (eg excavation on scheduled monuments for which permission was necessary, but no funds were granted). Successive seasons of work on the same site have been counted separately for each of the years in which they took place.

These figures show that excavation has always proved a more popular activity than publication. Nevertheless there has been a significant improvement in the rate of archaeological publication in recent years.

It is possible to chart this over a longer period, as publication lists have appeared in the Ancient Monuments Board Annual report each year since 1978. (AMB 1978–81).

Not only has the number of grant aided publications increased dramatically but the average size of these reports has almost doubled over the last ten years. In the period 1956–70 the average was around twenty-five pages per publication, but by the 1971–80 period this had risen to forty-two pages per publication.

There has also been a considerable increase in the standards of observation and reporting required. We now expect a higher level of objectivity and the recording of all the available information.

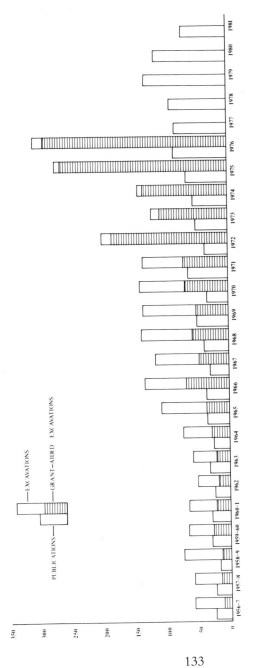

Fig. 8 Rescue excavations and publications which received assistance from the DoE, 1956–81.

Notes to Fig. 8

Sources: 1, IAM 1956–61: 2, MPBW 1962–69, DOE 1970–76: 3, AMB 1978–81. Publication lists for 1977 and 1978 have been extracted from the combined list (AMB 1978). Figures for excavation were not published in a format comparable with those above following the cessation of the Archaeological Excavations Annual Report series, and the formation of archaeological units.

133

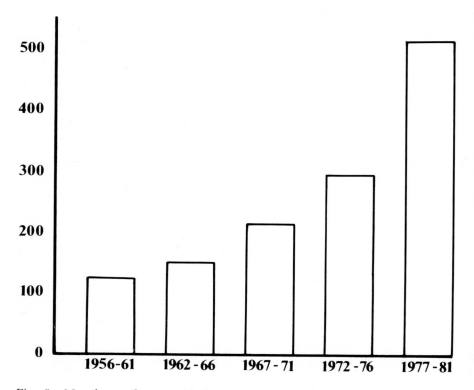

Fig. 9   Numbers of grant-aided publications in five-year periods, 1956–
1981.

Unfortunately even though there has been a significant rise in the number of people involved in archaeological work, as well as a rise in the number of reports published, there has not been a corresponding increase in the sale of these.

Publication outlets and finance

Traditionally publication of archaeological excavation reports has been financed in a number of ways. In the first place County and National societies have produced journals, usually annually, paid for out of membership subscriptions. Some of these have been published regularly since the 19th century. More recently it has become possible for the Department to assist the publication of reports on excavations it has grant aided and in some instances charitable institutions, business organisations and the British Academy and other bodies have also provided financial assistance.

However, as production costs have risen due to the twin spurs of inflation and more lengthy reporting, editors and subscribers have been forced to reconsider the need for the publication in printed form of some of the information contained in reports submitted to them.

Local journals in particular have felt consumer resistance, if their journals contained proportionately less of general interest to their members, and if the information which was published was more difficult to read and digest.

There has also been some resistance from excavators who have found that they either have difficulty in making available sufficient time to produce the detailed reports now required, or that their own records at the time of excavation were not suitable to supply the detail required, and who are thus detered from producing their results. It is therefore possible that there are at least some cases where by aiming at a higher standard of reporting we have unintentionally delayed access to useful information.

The converse of this is that many of the archaeologists who have used the more detailed recording methods now current, are unwilling to consider cutting down on the amount of information included in their final report. This reluctance may be understandable in view of the emphasis on complete reporting. Also publication is the conventional means of achieving recognition and status. However as Philip Rahtz pointed out (Grinsell, et al 1966 p. 38) quoting from Flinders Petrie's *'Methods and Aims in Archaeology'* (1904) p. 50–51 'To empty the contents of notebooks on a reader's head is not publication. A mass of statements which have no point, and do not appear to lead to any conclusion or generalisation, cannot be regarded as efficient publication.'

The revision of this (Grinsell et al 1974 p. 18) mentions the growing crisis in publication. More recently Professor Alcock (1980) has examined some of the reasons given for preferring traditional style reports, and he in fact dismisses most of them.

The following examples are a selection of the points he considers in 'The Purpose of Publication' Section 3 (Alcock 1980 p. 2–4).

'The most obvious reason for what may be called 'total publication' is to record, preserve, and disseminate information'. Other arguments include:

a) From the published account it should be possible to reconstruct the site on paper.

b) It should be possible to reinterpret the site from the published evidence.

c) It should be possible to judge the quality of the excavation and the excavator's skill, authenticate his recovery of data, and the inferences based on it.

He goes on to say that in fact 'there is no range of experience to show that it is possible to reinterpret a complex stratification', and the other arguments are also bogus. 'There is no way a reader can assess and verify the skill of the excavator from a published report'. 'It is impossible to know what the correct observations should have been'. 'We cannot judge an excavator's skill or awareness of his site from his own remarks, and it is quite unsatisfactory to base this on the internal evidence of the style of the report'.

'The upshot of all this is that the arguments advanced above are spurious, and we are forced back to the view that the purpose of publication is primarily to convey information. We should now tackle the problem of what information, and for whom'.

It is possible that archaeologists are still searching for a solution to publication problems because they oversimplify them, and do not recognise the conflict of interests involved.

It is difficult to see how the needs of the majority of county society members, who wish to have brief, interesting accounts of items of local interest, can be reconciled with the need of archaeologists to have reports published in full detail.

It is the editors of journals who are most frequently faced with resolving this conflict. They can only select items for publication from work submitted to them, but they have to be highly selective. They may lose subscribers if they undertake to publish long involved excavation reports too frequently.

In a situation where an editor was unable to accept a report which the Department was prepared to grant aid, and where there was no suitable alternative outlet, there is at present little that the Department can do to resolve the difficulty except arrange for a copy of the manuscript to be deposited with the National Monuments Record.

The origins of the 'Frere Report'

It was in response to some of the difficulties posed by this situation that the Rescue Committee of the Ancient Monuments Board set up a working party 'To consider the increasing delays in publishing definitive reports on archaeological rescue excavations, and with rapidly increasing publication costs in mind, the principles which should be followed in writing and editing reports' (AMB (1975) p ii).

The working party report was published in October 1975 as *'Principles of Publication in Rescue Archaeology'* (AMB 1975) commonly known as the 'Frere Report', after the chairman of the working party which produced it.

Much of the discussion in this report was concerned with the shortage of publication outlets, and most of the recommendations were concerned with remedying this shortage by establishing series of publications within the Department as well as encouraging societies to set up monograph series to cope with the larger reports being produced, (eg AMB 1975, 5 p. 9–11, but also 4.3 p. 7 on shortage of outlet and 3.4, 3.5 p. 8 on Department of the Environment publications).

Some of this has come to pass, but much has been overtaken by events, and in fact, while there may be some local difficulties, there is no reason to suppose that there is now a shortage of publication outlets. There are very few instances where existing manuscripts have not been published, and in many instances editors experience difficulty in obtaining completed work for publication. The Department's own series of HMSO monographs is frequently awaiting manuscripts which are overdue.

However some of the Frere Report recommendations have been official Department policy since 1976, and these are outlined below (see also Department of the Environment Advisory Notes 16. 25, 27, circulated to grant recipients).

Summary of the 'Frere' Principles

The report begins by reiterating the principle laid down in Curwen (1937 p. 6,) that 'everyone who by excavating destroys the evidence contained in the ground, undertakes the responsibility of *fully but concisely* restoring the evidence on paper'. (My italics).

The report continues 'We must constantly remind outselves that future generations of scholars will ask questions which cannot be anticipated today. For this reason mere preservation of significant results in non-published form is insufficient, but that publication in full detail has become an economic impossibility, for all but the smallest excavcations.' (AMB 1975, 2. 4, p. 2).

It therefore concludes 'that it will be necessary, in future, to consider a refined publication with synthesised descriptions, supporting data, selected finds and specialist reports, as the objective for all rescue excavation reports.' (AMB 1975 2. 6, p. 3).

In order to achieve these objectives a hierarchial organisation was suggested for the various levels of archaeological data which result from excavation, and the categories of evidence defined in levels I–IV:

Level I, this is the site itself, general notes, accounts of previous work, and excavated finds.
Level II, comprises the site note-books, on site recording forms, site drawings, primary finds records, x-rays, negatives, photographs, and any other records made during the course of the excavation.
Level III, is the processed complete archive consisting of description and full illustration of all structures and stratigraphic relationships, classified finds catalogues, finds drawings and detailed specialist reports.
Level IV, is the published report, which should contain an interpretative description of the site, together with evidence supporting the interpretation, selected finds, and summaries of specialist information.

It is stressed 'that the minimum acceptable standard of publication continues to be a full presentation of the history and significance of the site'. Nor is it acceptable to provide the evidence without any interpretation and discussion. It is emphasised that full documentation and evidence should be provided for all statements made. The interpretation should however be confined to matters relating to the site. Swollen comparative discussion should be avoided and general studies should normally seek independent publication (AMB 1975 2. 9 p. 3).

The Role of the 'Frere Report' in Department of the Environment Publication Policy

It is these aspects of the *'Principles of Publication in Rescue Archaeology'* (AMB 1975) which are applied by the Department to projects submitted to us for financial support.

It may be helpful when applying the scheme to think not of *levels*, but of *phases* of publication progress. In this way it can be seen that what is being suggested is an orderly programme of work, in which one process leads naturally on to the next, and where it will be necessary to have first reached phase III, before proceeding to phase IV.

The availability of microfiche techniques lends itself very well to this approach to the preparation of excavation records. It is now possible to provide a complete copy of the detailed report (Level III) with every copy of the printed text (Level IV). Fiche readers have become more readily available, and it is possible to obtain full size reproduction from fiche, from a number of sources. The difficulty anticipated by the 'Frere Report', in gaining access to stored archives, therefore no longer exists and the difficulty of trying to provide, on-demand, selected sections of the archive is also removed.

There is however an implied self-contradiction in the report, because as well as advocating archival treatment for some information it also states that 'mere preservation in a non-published form is insufficient' (AMB 1975 2. 4 p. 2). Use of fiche publication makes a significant contribution to resolving this difficulty 'in that it makes it possible for all necessary and relevant information to be made available' either as text or fiche in one package, at a substantial reduction over conventional publication costs.

It has been calculated from applications to the Department for publication grants that it costs between £20 – £40 to provide a printed page of information. Her Majesty's Stationery Office Reprographic Unit charged £3.85 (at October 1981 prices) to prepare a master fiche, which can contain up to 98 pages of text. The National Monument Record charged 25p (at June 1982 prices) for copies taken from master held by them. It has been calculated that the average cost of fiche for distribution with a report is currently (Summer 1982) about 6p per frame.

There has been some resistance to the application of the 'Principles of Publication' but as set out above they do provide a useful and organised approach to report writing which should be followed by anyone preparing a report with the aim of attracting a publication grant from the Department.

The concept of a carefully prepared archive has made it possible to sort out and present the mass of information generated currently by excavation and post-excavation processing techniques. Separation of the archive from the synthesised account of the site makes the whole report into a more coherent and intelligible body of information, without sacrificing access to the more detailed information for those who need it.

In considering the 'Frere Report' the two aims of the Working Party must be borne in mind (AMB 1975 1 p. 1). They were:

1) to resolve the delays in preparing reports,
2) to reduce the high cost of reproducing them.

While the application of microfiche technology to the archive will undoubtedly lead to a lessening in the cost of publishing large reports, unfortunately the requirement for a fully detailed archive may well have delayed the production of some reports, and has certainly extended the post-excavation process generally.

We should however be grateful to those who produced the 'Frere Report', for pointing out how to successfully lower the cost of our excavation reports, while at the same time allowing us not only to maintain our current standards of reporting, but actually to raise them and make every item of information available to everyone.

The above formed the basis of Department of the Environment publication policy.

Implementation – the Present

The role of the Department in archaeological work is confined to the preservation of source material for others to use as the basis of their research, and its promotion of archaeological publication must be governed by this.

Those archaeologists whose work it has grant aided are able to call on the following forms of assistance:

Post-excavation grants are usually made to assist with the processing of material, the preparation of the archive, and the typescript of the report.

Payments can also be made to specialist contributors for their reports.

Grants are made available to meet part of the printing and fiche production cost.

In addition a series of guidelines and advisory notes have been produced to give information on the standards and formats to be applied. These guidelines are usually based on the recommendations of working parties consisting of specialists and representatives of the Department. The guidelines produced generally represent a consensus of the views of all concerned and are intended to supply a suitable standard for work which it can grant-aid, although they usually also have a more general application. Examples are the 'Frere Report' itself (AMB 1975), the Central Excavation Unit paper, mentioned above (Jefferies 1977) Roman Pottery Guidelines (Young 1980) and Medieval Pottery guidelines (Blake and Davey 1983).

Implementation: The Future

It is now becoming increasingly clear that it is right to look at the present scale of assistance. Difficulties may be created in future by the fact that it takes relatively less time, effort and resources to prepare and publish the smaller, relatively less important excavations. The larger and more archaeologicaly significant reports can be delayed because of the greater time and resources needed to prepare and reproduce them. There is thus the possibility of the less important work, where results can be more quickly obtained gaining more than their fair share of available resources.

It is for this and other reasons that the Department is co-operating with a Council for British Archaeology in a joint working party to reconsider the publication requirements of the future. When the working party's report is available it will be submitted to the Ancient Monuments Board for consideration. It may then be necessary for the Directorate to reconsider its present policy in the light of the comments of the Ancient Monuments Board.

New Technology

In considering the application of new technology now emerging, it is recognised by the Department that numerical methods of recording and statistical analysis of numerical data are widespread, and that it is almost impossible to process this information beyond a certain scale, without access to computer technology. It is however extremely difficult for the Department to assist others in this area. In Publication Section we can only pay for work which will produce the final report, we cannot usually assist with large purchases of equipment on which to process information. We have in a small number of cases been able to grant aid the purchase of, or loan, microprocessors, but if lager scale or more sophisticated equipment is needed, this will depend on access negotiated through third parties such as Universities or Local Authorities. We can usually only support proposals for computer application when it can be shown that this will be cheaper than other methods of processing the material. We are unable to aid the development of new unproven applications.

In general the Department's attitude is in favour of the application of any new technique, or tool which will help with post-excavation work. However it does have to bear in mind that while it is interesting and exciting to be in the van of new developments, the rapid dissemination of the information is the most important consideration. The Department's aim in furthering the publication of reports on rescue excavations, is to provide as much information as possible, promptly and economically in order to make available the results of such excavations to the scholar and ultimately to enlarge the vision of the country's history for the general public.

Addendum

In the time that has elapsed since the preparation of this paper the joint

CBA/DOE working party has produced *The Publication of Archaeological Excavations*, known as 'the Cunliffe Report' after its chairman: this is now the basis of Departmental policy for the publication of archaeological excavations (DOE Advisory Note 40, Nov. 1983).

Bibliogrpahy
Ancient Monuments Board for England (AMB) 1975 *Principles of Publication in Rescue Archaeology* Report by a Working Party of the Ancient Monuments Board for England, Committee for Rescue Archaeology. DOE
Ancient Monuments Board for England (AMB) 1978–81 *Twenty-Fifth* to *Twenty-Eighth Annual Reports* HMSO
Alcock L. 1980 'Excavation and publication: some comments' *Proceedings of the Society of Antiquaries of Scotland* Vol 109 p 1–6
Blake H., Davey P. (1983) *Guidelines for the Processing and Publication of Medieval Pottery from Excavations* Directorate of Ancient Monuments and Historic Buildings Occasional Paper No 5 DOE
Curwen E. C. 1937 *The Archaeology of Sussex*
Department of the Environment (DOE) 1970–75 (Annually) *Archaeological Excavations* HMSO
Grinsell L., Rahtz P., Warhurst A. 1966 *The Preparation of Archaeological Reports*
Grinsell L., Rahtz P., Williams D. P. 1974 *The Preparation of Archaeological Reports* (Revised edition)
Inspectorate of Ancient Monuments (IAM) 1956–61 '*Excavations Sections Annual Report*' (IAM papers prepared annually for internal circulation)
Jefferies J. S. 1977 *Excavation Records: Techniques in use by the Central Excavation Unit* Directorate of Ancient Monuments and Historic Buildings Occasional Paper No 1 DOE
Ministry of Public Buildings and Works (MPBW) 1962–69 *Excavations Annual Report* HMSO Annually
Pitt-Rivers A. 1887–98 *Excavations in Cranbourne Chase* Vols 1–4
Young C. J. 1980 *Guidelines for the Processing and Publication of Roman Pottery from Excavations* Directorate of Ancient Monuments and Historic Buildings Occasional Paper No 4 DOE.

CHAPTER 15

PUBLICATION: CRISIS AND INACTION

Tom Hassall

Oxford Archaeological Unit

Standing Conference of Unit Managers

At the outset of this conference Henry Cleere, Director of the Council for British Archaeology, and I debated whether it was worse to give the first or the last paper. We both wanted to change places with each other. Being in our respective positions is rather like being the slices of bread on either side of a richly filled sandwich: certainly the quality of the filling has been outstanding this weekend.

I have been fascinated by all I have seen and heard, but, as a Unit Manager what I want to know and what I still feel has not been completely answered is the question: 'Information technology' – is it a Hit or a False drop?': you will note that I have at least acquired the jargon. The implications of information technology are enormous in management terms. Apart from the obvious interest in what the equipment can do the Unit Manager will also need to know who will provide the capital, how will recurring maintenance contracts be paid for and who will drive the machine? The options to the last question presented to us this weekend seem to range from a Micro Manager to an archaeological commune. The Unit Manager finds himself as always caught between what I used quaintly to call the upper and nether millstone, or what I suppose I should now call the interface between what is desirable for the discipline and what is financially possible.

The Oxford Unit has so far only put its toe into the bath of information technology. The unit's contacts are threefold. First, the unit has access to use of a mainframe. Although my unit is not a department of the Oxford University, it is an Associated Centre of St. Cross College. This College is a post-graduate college founded in 1965. Like all Oxford Colleges it is multi-disciplinary, but it is strong in the fields of computation and archaeology. I have a personal Fellowship at the College and this connection gives my research assistants and I access both to expertise within the

College and to the University mainframe. The unit is particularly indebted to the help of Susan Hockey who has indoctrinated unit staff into the mysteries of the mainframe and in particular she has helped Maureen Mellor with the program necessary for medieval pottery processing. Susan Hockey has also shown us the wonders of the University's Laser Comp. facilities whose implications for publication are dramatic.

The second area of contact has been involved with micro-computers. In 1978 Neil MacGavin directed an excavation of a Roman cemetery at Stanton Harcourt, and, thanks to the kind generosity of the Department of the Environment's Directorate of Ancient Monuments and Historic Buildings' (DAMHB) Central Excavation Unit, use was made of machine sorting of site data. The advantages of using a micro on our extensive programme of large DAMHB funded excavation projects became clear. The Department has provided the funds for the Unit to purchase a Research Machines 380Z. Jo Jefferies of the Central Excavation Unit is providing software which Phillip Page from the Unit is slightly modifying for our own requirements. The choice of machine was greatly influenced by the proven record of the 380Z, the fact that it was made and could be serviced in Oxford without expensive maintenance contracts, and because it appears to be the most widely used micro in Oxford University Departments. There is therefore a pool of local experience on which we can call. The exact uses to which our micro will be put, our working methods and its use in conjunction with the mainframe have yet to be defined. However apart from processing site and finds data it will be used as a word-processor, using Wordstar, and probably also for financial records. As an aside the Visicalc package appears to be the answer to the Unit Manager's prayer for help to work out the financial information expected of him by the DAMHB's insistence on Project Funding.

The third area of contact with the hardware of information technology concerns microfiche. The publication of archaeological material using fiche was largely pioneered by Peter Ashby of Oxford Microform. He persuaded the unit early on that dramatic savings could be made using fiche, and as I shall explain later the unit, in some cases reluctantly, has been preparing reports for some time with the use of fiche in mind. The unit owns its own fiche reader (a Microphax Vantage Com IV Reader fitted with an extension screen, carrier with D lens suitable for reports and an additional 'AA' lens suitable for 35mm plans) and its own reader printer, (a Bell and Howell 'Reporter').

The fact that the Oxford Unit has been dabbling with information technology is of course a reflection of my own unit's attempts to come to terms with data handling since the publication by the DAMHB of the Frere Report – *Principles of Publication in Rescue Archaeology*. It is the effect of this report on the work of the units since 1975 that I have been asked to discuss. That is the meaning which lurks behind the cryptic title of my paper.

When Henry Cleere opened the proceedings he told us that standing before this audience was rather like finding himself naked in Kensington

High Street. These are feelings with which I now all too readily sympathise. It would be easy enough for me to try to present a glowing picture of the world of units and my own in particular as being at the very heart of the White Hot Micro Revolution about which we have heard so much this weekend. But to do so would be to be blinded by the heat and light to the true facts of the situation. I stand before you naked and ashamed as the non-publishing director of a non-publishing unit. This personal 'crisis' in my life is just part of what is clearly a general crisis facing archaeological units throughout the country.

The crisis is of the units' own making and one which was perfectly predictable. The crisis is not simply one caused by the destruction of sites and the lack of resources to excavate them, but rather the reverse. It is a crisis caused by the large number of rescue excavations which have already taken place, and which have generated a vast mass of data to be analysed and disseminated. The backlog is now so great that it is preventing scarce resources from being applied to new excavations. Sites may therefore now be going unrecorded because of our own past successes and present failures. The simple answer would be further injections of funds. However DAMHB who in its present form or possible future guise would be the most likely single and most significant source of such funds does not see more money as the answer, even if it were available.

At a time when government funds are scarce it is suggested that the realistic answer cannot lie in additional funds but in a change of attitudes towards the processing and publications of excavations. What appears to be proposed is exactly analagous to the Government's theories or perhaps practise of the national economy. Units must not take on new rescue excavation commitments but must complete outstanding reports – a 'destocking' process to use economists' jargon. Thereafter, as human resources become available for excavation again, reports must be 'leaner and fitter'. This then is the crisis of my title and the 'inaction' is the apparent stagnation of post-excavation projects.

I want to examine the background to the present situation. I will obviously draw heavily on the particular experiences of the Oxford Unit, but some generalisations are necessary first of all. I must assume that the history of the way in which rescue units developed over the last fifteen years is a familiar story. I shall take for granted the original rescue archaeology crisis as part of the accepted history of archaeology. The multiplicity of organisations now involved with rescue archaeology is an integral part of the institutional archaeological landscape. These organisations take wildly different forms although they do have certain common denominators. DOE funds are crucial to their long-term existence. They have a community of interest which found its expressions in SCUM (the Standing Conference of Unit Managers), a deliberately chosen acronym in similar vein to KRAS and GOS. The present membership of SCUM is over eighty units, virtually every one in the country. While organisations may vary, ethics amongst these professional units are perhaps more uniform. There

144

can be few members of unit staffs who would not subscribe to paragraph 3.4 of the proposed Instutute of Field Archaeologists draft Code of Conduct which reads:

'An archaeologist shall ensure that the record resulting from his work is prepared in a *comprehensible, readily usable and durable form*'

The debate starts with the definition of '*comprehensible, readily usable and durable form*'.

The starting point of any discussion of definition must be the Frere Report. These principles were set out in Appendix II of this report:-

'The objective in publication of excavation reports should be to provide a synthesised description of the results, comprising a full presentation of the history and significance of the site, with full documentation and evidence for all statements made, and inclusion of all necessarily relevant material, such as selected pottery and small finds in their context. Secondary material where appropriate should be available on request. All original records of the fieldwork and post-excavation studies and data should be preserved for future reference in a permanent archive'.

Appendix I of the report contained a summary of recommended arrangements for storage and availability of excavation data. The Frere Report did not attempt close definitions or guidelines and therein lay its merit or its fatal flaw, depending on one's attitude. So far as the DAMHB was concerned the Frere Report became enshrined in its conditions of grant.

The DAMHB conditions of grant are amplified by DAMHB Advisory Notes. In the past these notes have been interpreted generously by our professional colleagues within the Department, but far less so of late. Administrators within the Department are at pains to emphasise that units are not expected to carry out research as such. In the words of the last Director of DAMHB the 'Department is in the business of preservation not excavation, we do not fund research'. Comments which cause a wry smile as units submit their research designs to the Department. But the conditions of grant have always made the position clear.

For the benefit of non DAMHB grant receivers it is worth recalling some of the constraints under which units produce reports. Thus for instance Advisory Note 16 (December 1978) lays down the Form of the Report:

'In order to qualify for a publication grant it is essential that the report should follow the recommendations of *Principles of Publication in Rescue Archaeology*, DOE 1975, especially those summarised in Appendix II (i). A draft or a detailed synopsis showing how the various classes of evidence will be treated should be submitted to the Inspectorate at an early stage in report preparation. Any subsequent alterations involving

145

significant revision must also be submitted. The final report, together with an index to the Level 3 archive, should be submitted to the Inspector or to a referee nominated by him, before being sent to an editor for publication. Failure to follow this procedure may result in the report being considered unsuitable for a publication grant.'

The 'flexible straight jacket' of Advisory Note 16 was reinforced in July 1980 by Advisory Note 25 on the Publication of Archaeological Reports. Apart from reiterating grant conditions it detailed the information required in synopses, demanded stricter application of the division between the Frere Report Levels 3 and 4, and emphasised the advantage of microfiche as a way of publishing large bodies of data cheaply.

The thinking behind these instructions was clear and it was given a more eloquent expression by M. W. Thompson when he addressed SCUM in 1980 in a paper entitled 'State Archaeology – Policies for the 1980s as seen from Wales'. He voiced the growing concern of DAMHB as follows:

'It is however in the treatment and handling of the great volume of material that is building up because of the size of rescue work that it seems to me the main advances can be made. It is by trying to shorten reports, cheapen the cost of publiction and mechanise or computerise the material that the main improvements are likely to be made. The present system of Government finance for reporting almost encourages the long reports and certainly does nothing to discourage them. This is an area that requires study preferably by someone who has no vested interest in long reports since they tend to simply urge spending more money! Indeed one of our main problems in rescue archaeology is to see and listen to dispassionate advice from people who are not too immersed in the matter to see the real issues.'

Professor Leslie Alcock may have provided just that dispassionate advice, at least as seen from the archaeological report reader's view rather than the compiler's viewpoint (Alcock 1980). He declared that the interests and needs of the consumer – that is the reader – should be paramount in publication. He went on:

'If this is accepted, then for the general reader, as well as for the university lecturer preparing his first year course on World Prehistory, or the museum curator designing an exhibit on the Bronze Age in Central Loamshire, the most that is needed is a summary account of major structures, most characteristic finds, and outline site history; with just enough presentation of the basic evidence to demonstrate how the main stratigraphic sequence is established and with the excavator's preferred solutions to all problems (structural, stratig-raphical, chronological etc), set out and justified as economically as possible. There will, in fact, be no time to read more. For a major site, the appropriate level of publication might be 40,000–50,000 words, with 100–120 figures and plates, in a hard-cover series; for a medium site, 5,000–10,000 words, 10–20 figures and plates, in national or county journal; for a minor site, a page in a county journal'.

The report as outlined above would still not be in Alcock's view the 'primary report.' This is still 'nothing less than the fullest possible description, analysis, discussion and illustration of the excavation evidence, structures, stratification, finds, environmental data etc.' therefore he stressed the need for a permanent, accessible and reproducible archive: 'the physical character of the primary report, as deposited in the archive, will closely resemble a conventional publication in a state of readiness for the printer'. This philosophy is fine from the reader's standpoint, it is fine from the point of view of those who have to fund and publish reports, but the units are still left with the problem of how and at what degree of depth to compile the 'primary report' and how to organise the archive.

However we have had to wait until January 1982 for the full extent of the problem to become clear. DAMHB under Geoffrey Wainwright's guidance has now spelt out for the first time the national situation. The information was contained in Wainwright's paper *An analysis of Central government (DAMHB) support in 1982/83 for the recording of archaeological sites and landscapes in advance of their destruction*. The paper, largely researched by Alison Allden, was presented at a seminar organised by the Prehistoric Society. Wainwright graphically portrayed the problem of units and publication in his Figure 7, from which the following statistics are taken:

	total bid%	total allocation%
Excavation	47%	26%
Post Excavation	38%	56%
Survey	7%	3%
Sites and Monuments	1%	2%
Aerial Photography	1%	2%
Overheads/Establishment	6%	11%

Wainwright's comments were:

'On the basis of these figures the Department's priority is clear – to publish what has already been excavated. However, it will also be apparent that to a degree this policy is contrary to that of the popular will as expressed by the bids we receive.... In all periods there is a dearth of new excavations or excavations in progress and an accumulation of projects in the list of those that are awaiting publication'

The new excavations exist but DAMHB has not got the budgetary flexibility to fund new projects because of the size of the total budget, and the 'apparent stagnation' of publication. Wainwright did not attempt to analyse the reasons, but he concluded:

> 'to some they will be methodical, to others financial and to some, no doubt, organisational. Perhaps the answer lies in a amalgam of all three. The conclusion, however is simple, solutions must be found and imposed, not only as a matter of professional ethics but also to retain professional credibility with those who hold the purse strings'.

Having sketched in the historical background as it affects units and publication, since the Frere report, I now want to turn to the specific example of the Oxford Archaeological Unit (OAU). In some respects the OAU is better off than many of its peers in that at least elements of the unit have been in the business longer than most other full-time rescue units. The unit which in its present form was founded in 1973 grew out of an amalgam of various bodies, such as the Oxford Archaeological Excavation Committee and the Upper Thames Archaeological Committee whose antecedents go back into the mists of time. However all the problems are still be be found with the OAU.

I believe that my own appointment as a full-time Director of the former Oxford Archeological Excavation Committee (OAEC) in 1967 was one of the first, if not the first full-time appointment to a Rescue Archaeology Unit *per se*. For practical and political reasons OAEC was originally conceived as conducting a five year operation with what by to-day's standards now seems a total lack of resources – one man and a bucket. The Oxford excavations themselves were concentrated to begin with in the St. Ebbe's area of the city. The largest single project was a three year series of excavations which took place before and during the construction of the Westgate shopping centre where a range of different sites was examined: domestic sites, streets, the city wall, the Oxford Greyfriars, the Castle and a medieval parish church. Large quantities of material were collected at a time when attitudes towards the collection of stratified material were changing radically. To give some idea of the scale of the problem something in the order of 55,000 stratified sherds of medieval pottery were retained, i.e. all stratified material. A former generation of archaeologists might well have discarded a high proportion of all but the most apparently 'significant' sherds. The realisation of the potential importance of post-medieval pottery was also gaining ground and a further 10,000 stratified sherds were retained. A similar post-excavation problem was acquired by the retention of all stratified animal bone.

It was originally assumed that after a 3 year period of excavation the post excavation work would take a further 2 years. With hindsight this was a wildly unrealistic estimate. While our future work methods may be streamlined, the unit's current experience would suggest that a Project Director is likely to spend a ratio of 1:3 in time spent on excavation and post-excavation work. This is assuming largely uninterrupted work time.

148

In practice my own time became increasingly involved with the overall administration of the unit; shortage of funds meant that it was impossible to offer continuity of employment of staff, while the staff themselves, myself included, were all young and lacking in post-excavation experience. When the appointment of full-time staff became possible the preference was for a full-time field officer, Brian Durham, who himself became committed to further excavation. The appointment of a pottery researcher came late in the day. The post is now held by Maureen Mellor who, as has already been said, has made a great deal of use of the Oxford University's mainframe computer to speed up her work.

The actual publication policy was to produce a series of interim reports in *Oxoniensia,* the county journal which was also thought of as the vehicle for all final reports. More recently interim notes have appeared in CBA Group IX *Newsletter,* since the *Newsletter* has more immediacy than *Oxoniensia* and space and finance is then liberated for final reports. So far as the final reports themselves are concerned it soon became apparent that in terms of work load it made much more sense to work on the well-stratified sites which could extend and tighten-up the form and fabric type sequence of Oxford's mid-Saxon to post-medieval pottery, rather than to write up the sites strictly in the order in which they were dug. Therefore the Westgate Centre sites were pushed back while sites under Oxford Castle, in St Aldate's (in the south suburb) and the Hamel (in the western suburb) were given priority. The former reports by myself (Hassall, 1976) and by Brian Durham (Durham, 1977) were basically conventional excavation reports, the latter by Nicholas Palmer (Palmer, 1980) saw the first use of microfiche. In our opinion the use of microfiche on this occasion was not really appropriate, since the report was designed to be the last conventional Oxford report and it was not designed for fiche. The use of fiche was insisted on by DAMHB in order to save printing costs; however, the additional staff time involved in preparing sections of the report for fiche together with the extensive costs of typing camera-ready as opposed to printer-ready copy probably negated the financial argument.

Subsequent Oxford reports are all being compiled with a view to the use of microfiche. The actual form of the reports will not be standardised, but the printed elements will explain what appear to be the most significant aspects of each site. The Oxford Greyfriars is a case in point. The report will form part of two large reports covering all the Westgate Centre sites. The reports will be divided into medieval and post-medieval sections to make the size more acceptable to *Oxoniensia.* For the medieval period the emphasis will be on the church with its virtually unique plan; almost everything else, including the table of the finds, will be on fiche. Conversely for the post-medieval period the discussion of the structure will be minimal and instead the report will concentrate on the fine stratified series of pit groups, a selection of which will be printed in full, but the main catalogue will be in fiche.

Thus in Oxford we are still trying to cope with a backlog while taking on new projects as well. I suspect that the Oxford experience is analogous to the position that many other units find themselves in. However with the unit's projects in the new County of Oxfordshire the situation is probably healthier so far as work flow is concerned. The unit began its work in the county in 1973 when it was founded as an amalgamation of all those bodies, like the Oxford Archaeological Excavation Committee, who were already carrying out rescue excavations in the county. Many of the problems that we have already seen in the city are to be found in the county, for example, basically ill-paid and young staff (although we are all growing old together), learning old and new techniques. The crucial difference has been that in theory when a Field Officer takes on a new project he is then expected to write it up rather than take on new large commitments. We have therefore seen something approaching a steady flow of reports. The reports themselves are published in one of three publications. The unit's Annual Report is published in CBA Group IX *Newsletter.*In this Report, apart from the interim accounts already referred to, small final reports are also published. The sites which are published here are usually those only worth a short note with possible greater detail housed in the county Sites and Monuments Record. Medium sized reports are published in *Oxoniensia* while the largest reports which would swamp the county journal have been published as CBA research reports. For our purposes it is these last reports which are perhaps most worth considering.

The two reports so far published with CBA (Parrington, 1978 and Lambrick and Robinson, 1979) both broke new ground so far as methodology is concerned, with regard to the environmental evidence. This fact is reflected in both reports but particularly in the Farmoor report. Environmental methodology is discussed at length in both reports and therefore the reports are longer than subsequent sites with similar potential.

It is however the next report that is perhaps of more general interest. This is the report of David Miles on the multi-period site at Barton Court Farm, Abingdon (Miles, forthcoming). This report is very different from any of the unit's preceeding reports since it was designed with a view to text/fiche from the start. The form of this report is best seen in the synopsis of the Printed and Fiche Elements which are given as Appendix A of this paper. From the synopsis it will be seen that the report's printed section contains a series of chapters which are very much a discussion and synthesis of the evidence. This section of the report should be able to stand in its own right and be read without reference to the supporting data. The supporting data are all contained within the fiche. The fiche section appears much more like a conventional excavation report, although the finds section differs from other Oxford unit reports in that it is arranged on a functional basis.

You the consumers will have to judge the merits of the report. However I would explain that from the point of view of finance, while this report cost much less to print than its predecessors it certainly did not cost less to prepare. It is of course also only one model, and within the unit views as to the form of the perfect report vary wildly. No other reports currently in preparation exactly follow the Barton Court Farm model.

We will clearly see in the future different ways of producing syntheses of reports and the use of microfiche but I want to turn finally to Professor Alcock's ideas of publishing no detailed data at all. This brings up again the whole question of the archive. We all know what an archaeological archive can look like – a scruffy heap of site notebooks stored in a cardboard box. But it is in this area that I believe that the profession must radically alter its attitudes. Again i must hasten to add that the Oxford unit is not a model in this respect. But the archive whether on paper, film, magnetic tape or fiche should not be treated as a dustbin, as can happen. We must give much more serious thought to its storage, and I would suggest to such basics as to how archives should be catalogued, how the contents should be referred to and how museums are going to curate archives. It may be because I have a formal academic training as an historian and worked for a short while with the Victoria County History that it seems to me that archaeologists need to debate soon and seriously quite straightforward aspects of archives.

The Oxford unit's archives have been put on microfiche by the National Monuments Record as part of a pilot scheme, but which of course has now become a condition of DAMHB grant. In discussion with Alan Aberg of NMR we realised the need to order our archive in a usable form which would make sense from the point of view of the fiche and provide a reference system. George Lambrick from the unit compiled a catalogue system for the Oxford Blackfriars. The system is given in Appendix B. The NMR has been using this system as a model for some other unit archives but I would be interested to hear of other unit's experiences or suggestions for modifying our system.

Finally, if units have failed to deliver the goods in the post Frere Report era, much of the blame must rest with managers of units, like myself. The root of the problem is probably that while we are Project orientated, and DAMHB now accepts the need for Excavation Research Designs at the outset of the excavation, we have not yet turned our attention to equally well-worked out Publication Research Designs. The DAMHB grant conditions have moved somewhat in that direction, but not so firmly as I think will be necessary. In future Project Directors, with their Unit Manager and all the associated specialists involved in archive and published report preparation, must set out clearly what they consider to be the significant aspects of all elements of a given site, and have the professional courage and acumen to recognise what is not worth publishing.

Perhaps in 1984 it should really be a case of 'published and be damned'. It would be a fine irony if the future sign of success of an archaeologist should be a deliberate policy of non-publication in the conventional sense of the term. In other words professional advancement and success in the future, just as in practice for many of us in the past, may depend on non-publication, but deliberate non-publication backed up by a total and readily accessible archive – and therein lies the difference.

Bibliography

Alcock, L. 1980 Excavation and publication: some comments. *Proceedings of the Society of Antiquaries of Scotland* 109, 1977–8, 1–6

Durham, B. G. 1977 Archaeological investigations in St Aldate's, Oxford. *Oxoniensia* 42, 83–203

Hassall, T. G. 1976 Excavations at Oxford Castle, 1965–73 *Oxoniensia* 41, 232–308

Lambrick, G. and Robinson, M. 1979 *Iron Age and Roman Riverside Settlements at Farmoor, Oxfordshire.* CBA Research Report 32

Miles, D.(ed) forthcoming *Archaeology at Barton Court Farm, Abingdon, Oxon.* CBA Research Report 50

Palmer, N. 1980 A Beaker burial and Medieval tenements in the Hamel, Oxford. *Oxoniensia* 45, 124–225

Parrington, M. 1978 *The excavation of an Iron Age Settlement, Bronze Age ring-ditches and Roman features at Ashville Trading Estate, Abingdon (Oxfordshire) 1974–6.* CBA Research Report 28

APPENDIX A

Archaeology at Barton Court Farm Abingdon, Oxon, ed David Miles, CBA Research Report 50, forthcoming.

Contents

Printed Element

1. Introduction: Acknowledgements
2. Contents of Fiche
3. Geography of Barton Court Farm
4. Synopis of Excavation Report
5. Barton Court Farm: its landscape and resources
6. The nuclei of ancient farming: settlement activities
7. Trade and Affluence: the farm's contacts with the outside world
8. Continuity and change
9. Implications and future research
10. Bibliogrpahy

Fiche Element

1. Printed element
2. Site geography: geology, soils, climate, water supply, setting
3. i)   Neolithic – Finds by Alistair Whittle
    ii)   Late Iron Age – David Miles (DM)
    iii)   Early Romano-British – DM
    iv)   Late Romano-British – DM
    v)   Saxon – Saxon Finds – D. Brown
    vi)   Post Medieval Finds
4. Human Burials – Mary Harman & DM
5. C14 dating
6. Finds Report: organised on functional basis
    i)   Agriculture, crafts and industries
        a)   Wool gathering – Bill Manning
        b)   Textile equipment – Gwyn Miles
        c)   Leather working – DM
        d)   Netting – DM
        e)   Bone working – DM
        f)   Milling – R. J. Spain
        g)   Quernstones – DM

ii)   Coin report – C. E. King
iii) Building materials and tools
    a)   Stone and wall plaster – DM
    b)   Nails – Bill Manning
    c)   Tools – Bill Manning
    d)   Window glass – Jennifer Price
iv)   Personal equipment
    a)   Shoes – J. H. Thornton, Wendy Page & DM
    b)   Brooches – C. Harding
    c)   Buckles & belt fittings – Bill Manning
    d)   Pins – DM
    e)   Beads – DM
    f)   Rings – DM
    g)   Bracelets – DM
    h)   Combs – Valerie de Hoog
    i)   Games counters – DM
v)   Religious objects
    a)   A miniature bronze anchor – Miranda Green
    b)   Perforated oyster shell – DM
vi)   Weapons and hunting gear – Bill Manning
vii) Domestic and household equipment
    a)   Keys and latches – Bill Manning
    b)   Mounts and bindings – Bill Manning
    c)   Jet Plaque – Martin Henig
    d)   Bronze mounts – DM
    e)   Weights and measures – DM
    f)   Sewing – DM
    g)   Ladles and knives – Bill Manning
    h)   Whetstones – DM
    i)   Miscellaneous objects – DM
    j)   Vessels of bronze, shale, wood and glass – J. Price & DM

7. The Pottery: Iron Age, Roman and Saxon – DM with D. Hofdahl & J. Moore

8. The Bone Report – Bob Wilson with, Fish – Alwyne Wheeler, Birds – Don Bramwell, Cattle Horn Cores – Philip Armitage

9. Carbonised Plants – Martin Jones

10. Waterlogged Biological Material
    i)   Pollen – J. R. A. Greig
    ii)   Mosses – J. H. Dickson
    iii) Other plants – Mark Robinson
    iv)   Insects – Mark Robinson

11. Crop Plants: discussion – Martin Jones & Mark Robinson

12. Towards a Model of the Roman estate – Martin Jones.

APPENDIX B

Oxford Archaeological Unit Archives: Proposed cataloguing system compiled by George Lambrick

1. All archives must have a detailed catalogue of what is in them and where it is stored, along with details of where all other material from the site is stored: without this the whole idea of archival accessibility is pointless.
2. Anyone using the archive will normally start from a report, and therefore the archive must relate to the report in the use of numbering systems etc. in such a way that anything may easily be found. The report should be the first item in the archive so that it is available for ready reference, and if necessary it should be annotated to facilitate access to the records.
3. The designation of different categories of information (Appendix C) reflects two principal factors:
   a) the progess of how the archive material accumulates – *viz.* written site records, drawings and photographs; recording/analysis of different materials recovered; preparation of reports; the continuous accumulation of correspondence and other less archaeologically relevant material.
   b) the physical difference between different types of record and their consequent different storage systems – e.g. notebook/context sheet drawings and site plans; working drawings (to be consulted) and publication drawings (only to be handled for republication); photographs and paper records.

   The attached list of categories is a slight revision of the original proposals used for Blackfriars, Farmoor etc. The sort of material that might be put in each category is also given.
4. The numbering system for each category is a modified form of standard archive numbering, *viz.* upper case letters, lower case letters, upper case Roman numerals, lower case Roman numerals, arabic numerals.

   e.g. B/d/I/iii/3

   What sub-categories are made will depend entirely on how the information is most usefully grouped, which should be self-evident to the compiler of the archive who will know how much and what is to be included. Five subdivisions seems adequate (so far) within one site, but

155

it may be necessary to add a museum accession number at the beginning before the archive is transferred. The sub-categories do not rigidly indicate the status of the information, so what is used to enumerate individual items depends on how many subdivisions have already been made. However, it may be preferred always to use arabic numerals for the lowest subdivision of the material, especially in categories with large numbers of individual items such as photographs and plans.

The advantages of hierarchial numbering are important:

a) it makes it much easier for the researcher to identify which body of archive he needs to consult.

b) it allows items to be added in their logical place without disrupting the rest of the numbering (the idea of a 'complete' or 'final' archive seems to be a myth).

5. The need for additional cross-referencing should be considered by testing the archive's capacity for retrieving information. Obviously almost endless cross-referencing (e.g. between beetles and section drawings or pottery and plans etc. etc.) is theoretically possible, but it is very doubtful whether it is worth the effort. On the whole excavation records have a built-in cross-reference system in the context number: moreover if good records have been kept and they are well organised and adequately listed and catalogued additional references should not be required. If they are, a list of references arranged by subject and context should be appended to the main archive catalogue.

6. Microfiche copies of the site archives are to be held by the unit and the NMR in London. So far the indexing of the fiches has not been ideal. Preferably they should be numbered consecutively within categories *and* they should give the catalogue number of the first and last item on each fiche (if the catalogue number is the same, as in pottery record sheets or context sheets, the relevant context number should also be given). As at present a new fiche should begin each main category. Fiche numbers would thus be A1, A2, A3, B1, B2 etc. When the fiches have been made it will be necessary to cross-reference the individual fiche numbers with the main catalogue, and a paper copy of the main catalogue must be stored with each set of fiches (the *fiche* copy of the catalogue is obviously of little use to someone who constantly wants to refer to different items, unless it can be projected simultaneously).

There is a problem in adding new material to the fiche archive as it cannot be slotted in as in the paper archive, but if main categories begin on new fiches as at present it is at least possible to add material in the right overall category: obviously the paper catalogue with the fiches would also need amending.

156

Since the microfiche copies will become the unit's copy of the archive (as currently proposed) it is obviously vital that it should be adequately catalogues and indexed: the paper catalogue will need to show not only where each fiche begins in the catalogues of items in the archive, but also at which frame number on which fiche each item occurs. Each item would thus be given the fiche number followed by the frame number e.g. B4m9. Initially at least it is members of the unit who are likely to be the main (if not sole) users of the archive, and since the unit copies will be microfiches it is in our own interests to ensure they are properly indexed.

7. The transferring of the main archive of a site should not be done until it is as complete as possible: it and its fiches must be fully catalogued and adequate cross-referencing must be included; copies of documents (such as Carbon 14 certificates) and photographs (e.g. slides and negatives) of direct archaeological relevance which are to be retained by the unit must be included; all finds and other material must have been properly sorted, catalogued, indexed and stored; as much relevant original documentation (or copies of it) as possible must be extracted from specialists and included in its proper place. It is the responsibility of excavation directors to ensure that their archives are in a fit state to be handed over.

APPENDIX C

Oxford Archaeological Unit Archives: categories for proposed cataloguing system

A. Report(s): e.g. final published report; published and otherwise circulated interim reports; spin-off articles; etc.

B. Site Data: e.g. context notebooks/sheets; level books; site records of section, plan, photograph, sample nos. etc; non-excavational survey records e.g. fieldwalking, building survey; lists and guides to contexts for preparation of specialist finds and other reports; notes and diagrams of stratigraphy; lists of contexts by phase; etc.

C. Large non-publication drawings: e.g. catalogue of all large non-publication drawings; site plans and large sections; non-excavational drawings e.g. fieldwalking plans, building survey; copies of proposed development plans; stratigraphy flow diagrams; copies of publication drawings; plans from documentary data.

D. Photographs: e.g. detailed catalogue of all photographs; site slides b/w negs. and prints; finds photographs; other photographs such as copies of old photos, press photographs; cine film; miscellaneous prints.

E. Finds data: e.g. catalogues and lists of finds by context; indexes of storage locations; small find lists or cards; record sheets; unpublished analyses; small unpublished/draft drawings.

F. Environmental data: eg. sample information; lists of preserved samples and specimens and their location; record sheets; notes on methodology; unpublished analyses; small unpublished drawings.

G. Documentary material: e.g. copies of documents; lists of references; unpublished analyses and notes; small unpublished/draft drawings; etc.

H.	Human remains data:	e.g. lists by context; index of storage location record sheets; unpublished analyses; small sized unpublished/draft drawings; etc.
I.	Draft reports:	e.g. manuscript and typescript drafts; final typescript notes; references; proofs; etc.
J.	Publication drawings:	e.g. published drawings for reports plus spin-off articles; other drawings of publication standard for possible future use.
K.	Public relations:	e.g. material for exhibitions/open days; press cuttings; etc.
L.	Finances:	e.g. miscellaneous financial papers not included in DAU main files; etc.
M.	Correspond-ence:	e.g. all correspondence relating to site except that containing direct archaeological 'in-formation which is put in the relevant main section; and that concerning finances which is kept in OAU main files.
N.	General miscellaneous:	e.g. anything which cannot be categorized in one of the above sections – notes/reports on other related sites; parallels etc.; reviews; ephemera.

Each category may be subdivided in a hierarchy of categories denoted by: lower case letters, upper case Roman numerals, lower case Roman numerals and arabic numerals, e.g. B/d/I/iii/3.